Praise for
Chase the Lion

"*Chase the Lion* is a powerful, passion[...] [...] you pursue God's dream for your life, it can be a little scary, but man is it worth it!"
—TIM TEBOW

"Creative. Inspiring. Challenging. Batterson's writings always leave us encouraged, and *Chase the Lion* is no exception. If you feel as if life has caused you to shrink the size of your dreams, this book is for you!"
—LOUIE GIGLIO, pastor of Passion City Church, founder of Passion Conferences, and author of *The Comeback*

"Mark Batterson reminds us to trust in the powerful truth that with God we don't have to let our thinking be limited. By obeying Him, we let our growing faith push us to dream big and lean in ever closer to Him without fear or hesitation. It's time to trust in our God, who allows us to accomplish things that seem bigger than we could ever imagine!"
—CRAIG GROESCHEL, pastor of Life.Church and author of *#Struggles: Following Jesus in a Selfie-Centered World*

"We seek out community in everything we do—and our dreams should be no different. In *Chase the Lion,* Batterson reminds us to come together, share our dreams, and chase after them. And in doing so, we become not only dream chasers but dream catchers for the others in our pride."
—STEVEN FURTICK, pastor of Elevation Church and *New York Times* best-selling author

"Pastor Mark has done it again! This is a must-read for anyone who has ever felt discouraged or disappointed. *Chase the Lion* not only helped me take a fresh look at my life's purpose, but it also gave me the renewed energy to dream big and work hard. Pastor Mark is truly gifted at making God's Word accessible and encouraging."
—MARA SCHIAVOCAMPO, *Good Morning America* correspondent

"*Chase the Lion* fosters an expansive mind-set that drives our willingness to dream bigger than ever before. This mind-set is a choice, a decision, and a belief that God designed and created each of us for greatness, nothing less. If we aren't courageous and bold enough to extend ourselves and believe that God will give us the capacity for greatness, we will have cheated our potential. This book is for anyone scared of not achieving the real greatness they are capable of."

—BUZZ WILLIAMS, head basketball coach at Virginia Tech

"Mark Batterson's writing has had a profound impact on my life, both personally and professionally. Join me in accepting Mark's challenge to pursue a dream so big that only God can turn it into a reality. Life is better when you're chasing lions!"

—KIRK COUSINS, quarterback for the Washington Redskins

"Mark's books have inspired me and helped me to inspire our team. Straight from God's Word, *Chase the Lion* is a great message for any team and for people in every walk of life."

—JOHN HARBAUGH, head coach of the Baltimore Ravens

"Mark Batterson is an outstanding voice among the emerging generation of pastors in the US. He has much wisdom to offer anyone who wants to draw closer to Jesus, combining brilliantly the vision and clarity of a pioneer with the warmth and kindness of a pastor."

—NICKY GUMBEL, vicar of Holy Trinity Brompton

"I just finished *Chase the Lion* and am in tears, in awe of how my God created me to be a warrior for His great name. Mark's words force me to ask and answer: What lions am I chasing? What dreams am I dreaming that will make a difference in my children and my children's children and a hundred years from now?"

—HUGH FREEZE Jr., head football coach at the University of Mississippi

CHASE
THE
LION

**If Your Dream Doesn't Scare You,
It's Too Small**

Mark Batterson

MULTNOMAH

CHASE THE LION

Italics in Scripture quotations reflect the author's added emphasis.

Details in some anecdotes and stories have been changed to protect the identities of the persons involved.

Trade Paperback ISBN 978-1-60142-887-5
Hardcover ISBN 978-1-60142-885-1
eBook ISBN 978-1-60142-886-8

Cover design by Mark D. Ford; photography by Keith Ladzinski / Getty Images

Published in association with the literary agency of The Fedd Agency, Inc., P.O. Box 341973, Austin, TX 78734.

Published in the United States by Multnomah, an imprint of the Crown Publishing Group, a division of Penguin Random House LLC, New York.

MULTNOMAH® and its mountain colophon are registered trademarks of Penguin Random House LLC.

Originally published in hardcover in the United States by Multnomah, an imprint of the Crown Publishing Group, a division of Penguin Random House LLC, New York, in 2016.

The Library of Congress has cataloged the hardcover edition as follows:
Names: Batterson, Mark, author.
Title: Chase the lion : if your dream doesn't scare you, it's too small / Mark Batterson.
Description: First Edition. | Colorado Springs, Colorado : Multnomah, 2016. | Includes bibliographical references.
Identifiers: LCCN 2016021278 (print) | LCCN 2016026686 (ebook) | ISBN 9781601428851 (hard cover) | ISBN 9781601428868 (electronic)
Subjects: LCSH: Bible. Samuel, 2nd, XXIII—Criticism, interpretation, etc. | Benaiah (Biblical figure)
Classification: LCC BS1325.52 .B378 2016 (print) | LCC BS1325.52 (ebook) | DDC 248.4—dc23
LC record available at https://lccn.loc.gov/2016021278

Printed in the United States of America
2020—Trade Paperback Edition

10 9 8 7

SPECIAL SALES
Most Multnomah books are available at special quantity discounts when purchased in bulk by corporations, organizations, and special-interest groups. Custom imprinting or excerpting can also be done to fit special needs. For information, please e-mail specialmarketscms@penguinrandom house.com or call 1-800-603-7051.

To the Lion Chasers
You have faced your fears and chased your dreams.
Keep running to the roar!

CONTENTS

The Lion Chaser's Manifesto

Quit living as if the purpose of life
is to arrive safely at death.
Run to the roar.
Set God-sized goals. Pursue God-given passions.
Go after a dream that is destined to fail
without divine intervention.
Stop pointing out problems. Become part of the solution.
Stop repeating the past. Start creating the future.
Face your fears. Fight for your dreams.
Grab opportunity by the mane and don't let go!
Live like today is the first day and last day of your life.
Burn sinful bridges. Blaze new trails.
Live for the applause of nail-scarred hands.
Don't let what's wrong with you
keep you from worshiping what's right with God.
Dare to fail. Dare to be different.
Quit holding out. Quit holding back. Quit running away.

Chase the lion.

CHASE THE LION

On a snowy day, he chased a lion down into a pit and killed it.

2 Samuel 23:20, NLT

WHEN THE IMAGE OF A man-eating beast travels through the optic nerve and into the visual cortex, the brain relays an urgent message to the body: *run!* That's what normal people do, but normal is overrated. Lion chasers don't run away; lion chasers run to the roar. They don't see a five-hundred-pound problem; they seize opportunity by the mane. They don't take flight; they fight to the death for their dreams.

Buried in the second book of Samuel, the twenty-third chapter and the twentieth verse, is one of the most counterintuitive acts of courage in all of Scripture. It's just 1 of 31,102 verses in the Bible, but it's my personal favorite. It's little more than a biblical byline, but it's become the storyline of my life. My life motto is encapsulated in its message—*chase the lion.*

> There was also Benaiah son of Jehoiada, a valiant warrior from Kabzeel. He did many heroic deeds, which included killing two champions of Moab. Another time, on a snowy day, he chased a lion down into a pit and killed it.[1]

Napoleon Bonaparte made a distinction between two kinds of courage—*regular courage* and *two-o'clock-in-the-morning courage.* "The rarest attribute among Generals," said the Little Corporal, "is two o'clock-in-the-morning courage."[2]

Chasing a lion into a pit on a snowy day takes two-o'clock-in-the-morning courage. But that one act of courage completely changed the trajectory of Benaiah's life. The same is true of you. You are one idea, one risk, one decision away from a totally different life. Of course, it'll probably be the toughest decision you ever make, the scariest risk you ever take. But if your dream doesn't scare you, it's too small.

Scripture doesn't explain what Benaiah was doing or where he was going when he crossed paths with the lion. We don't know the time of day or his frame of mind. But it does reveal his gut reaction, and it was gutsy.

Put yourself in Benaiah's sandals.

Your vision is obscured by falling snow and frozen breath. Out of the corner of your eye, you detect movement. Pupils dilate. Muscles flex. Adrenaline rushes. It's a prowling lion stalking its prey—you.

In the wild, man versus lion scripts the same way every time. Man runs; lion chases; king of the beasts eats manwich for lunch. But Benaiah flips the script. That's what courage does! I don't know if it was the look in his eye or the spear in his hand, but the lion turns tail and Benaiah gives chase.

A fully grown lion can run thirty-six miles per hour and leap thirty feet in a single bound. Benaiah doesn't stand a chance, but that doesn't keep him from giving chase. He can't keep pace, but he can track paw prints in the freshly fallen snow. He comes to the place where the ground has given way beneath the lion's five-hundred-pound frame. Benaiah peers into the pit. Yellow cat eyes glare back.

It's a made-for-Hollywood moment. Imagine it on the silver screen.

Benaiah walks away from the pit while moviegoers breathe a sigh of relief. But Benaiah isn't walking away; he's getting a running start. The audience gasps as Benaiah turns around and takes a flying leap of faith, disappearing into the darkness. A deafening roar echoes off the walls of the cavernous pit, followed by a bloodcurdling battle cry.

Then silence, dead silence.

No one is eating popcorn at this point.

Everyone expects the lion to strut out, shaking its mane. But no. A human form reaches up and climbs out of the pit. Drops of blood color the snow crimson. Claw marks crisscross Benaiah's spear arm. But against all odds, the valiant warrior from Kabzeel earns an epic victory.

Closing credits roll.

Then, if I'm producing the film, there is a postcredit scene like in the *Marvel* superhero movies—Benaiah's cage fight with a giant Egyptian.[3]

Chase the Lion

If you find yourself in a pit with a lion on a snowy day, you've got a problem. Probably the last problem you'll ever have! But you've got to admit, "I killed a lion in a pit on a snowy day" looks awfully impressive on your résumé, especially if you're applying for a bodyguard position with the king of Israel.

Benaiah not only landed his dream job as King David's bodyguard, but his life exceeded his wildest dreams. Benaiah climbed the military chain of command all the way to the top, becoming commander in chief of Israel's army. The lion chaser became the most powerful person in the kingdom of Israel, save the king. But the genealogy of his dream traces back to a fight-or-flight moment. One decision determined his destiny. And not much has changed in the three millennia since then. You can run away from what you are afraid of, but you'll be running the rest of your life. It's time to face your fears, take a flying leap of faith, and chase the lion!

In every dream journey there comes a moment when you have to quit living as if the purpose of life is to arrive safely at death. You have to go after a dream that is destined to fail without divine intervention.

You have to go big or go home.

You have to take the road less traveled or settle for status quo.

You have to bite the bullet or turn your back on your dreams.

I have a theory: *your favorite scripture will become the script of your life.* I take my cues from 2 Samuel 23:20. That script underscores who I want to be, what I want out of life, and what I believe about God. *Chase the lion* is more than a nice catch phrase; it's the metanarrative of my life.

Most of us spend our lives running away from the things we're afraid of. We forfeit our dreams on the altar of fear. Or we chase after the wrong things. We're so busy climbing the ladder of success that we fail to realize it's leaning against the wrong wall.[4]

At the end of our lives, our greatest regrets will be the God-ordained opportunities we left on the table, the God-given passions we didn't pursue, and the God-sized dreams we didn't go after because we let fear dictate our decisions.

No Guts, No Glory

Most people believe God is real, but few people actually live like it. The result is a widening gap between their theology and their reality. They allow their circumstances to get between them and God instead of letting God get between them and their circumstances. Lion chasers measure everything against almighty God, including five-hundred-pound lions. That's the difference between being a scaredy-cat and a lion chaser.

When everything is said and done, God isn't going to say, "Well said," "Well thought," or "Well planned." There is one measuring stick: "Well done, good and faithful servant!"[5]

Faithfulness is not holding down the fort.

Faithfulness is chasing five-hundred-pound lions.

There is a brand of religiosity that seems satisfied with breaking even— *don't do this, don't do that, and you'll be okay.* The problem with that is this: you can do nothing wrong and still do nothing right. Breaking even is breaking bad. God has called us to play offense with our lives. Those who simply run away from what's wrong will never amount to more than half Christians. The only way to tap your God-given potential, to fulfill your God-ordained destiny is to chase five-hundred-pound lions.

God's dream for your life is so much bigger, so much better than breaking even. If you focus on not making mistakes, you won't make a difference. You don't overcome sin by focusing on *not* sinning. You need a dream that is bigger and better than the temptations you're trying to overcome. You need a dream that doesn't allow you to become spiritually sidetracked, a dream that demands your utmost for His highest.[6]

There is an old aphorism: *No guts, no glory.* When we lack the guts to go after five-hundred-pound lions, we rob God of the glory He deserves. By definition, a God-sized dream will be beyond your ability, beyond your resources. Unless God does it, it can't be done! And that is precisely how God gets the glory. He does things we can't do so we can't take credit for them. God honors big dreams because big dreams honor God.

Destiny is not a mystery. Destiny is a decision—a difficult decision, a daring decision, a counterintuitive decision. You fulfill your destiny one opportunity at a time. Of course, those opportunities often come disguised as five-hundred-pound problems. Landing in a pit with a lion on a snowy day qualifies as a bad day, a bad break. But Benaiah didn't see it as bad luck; he saw it as his big break.

If you're looking for an excuse, you'll always find one.

If you're looking for an opportunity, you'll always find one.

Lion chasers have an eye for opportunity. There are amazing opportunities all around us all the time, but you have to see them to seize them. Then you need two-o'clock-in-the-morning courage to chase them.

The Genesis of a Dream

When I was nineteen years old, I heard a sermon that would change the trajectory of my life. Sam Farina preached about a man named Benaiah, who chased a lion into a pit on a snowy day. I had never heard the story, and I could barely believe it was in the Bible. But a thought fired across my synapses: *If I ever write a book, I'd like to write a book about that verse.* That was the genesis of a dream titled *In a Pit with a Lion on a Snowy Day.*

It would take sixteen years for that dream to become reality, and I almost gave up on it a time or two. On October 16, 2006, *In a Pit* released with very little fanfare. In fact, it almost didn't see its second printing. But *In a Pit* beat the odds and inspired a generation of lion chasers to go after their dreams. Ten years later *In a Pit* has a sequel: *Chase the Lion.*

I'm often asked which of my books is my favorite. You might as well ask me which one of my children is my favorite! I love them all, but there is something unique about seeing your firstborn book on a bookshelf for the first time. *In a Pit* isn't my best-selling book, but if the measuring stick is life-altering decisions directly resulting from reading it, it might get the grand prize. It's been a game changer for lots of lion chasers, and I'll share some of their dream journeys in *Chase the Lion.* Their dreams are as different as they are, but each one has chased a lion in his or her own unique way. I hope their five-hundred-pound dreams inspire you as much as they have me.

In the prequel to this book, I focused exclusively on King David's bodyguard, Benaiah. *Chase the Lion* is the rest of the story. Like Washington's inner circle or Lincoln's team of rivals, David's thirty-seven mighty men rank as a most remarkable band of brothers. They were insanely courageous, fiercely loyal. Their exploits would be unbelievable if they weren't recorded in Scripture. And without them, David's dream of becoming king would have died a fugitive's death.

Our destiny is more intricately interwoven with others than any of us realize. The goal of *Chase the Lion* isn't simply to help you discover *your* dream. The best way to discover your dream is to help other people accomplish theirs! That's what the mighty men did, and in so doing, their lives surpassed their wildest dreams.

That's my prayer for you.

May you discover *your God-sized* dream in the pages of this book, and may you have the courage to chase it. But your greatest legacy isn't your dream; it's the dreams you inspire in others! You aren't just a dreamer; you are a dreamcatcher.

As you begin this dream journey, don't go it alone. Dreamers love company! Chase the lion with a friend, a spouse, a mentor. Form a pride, just as lions do. Together you can accomplish far more than the sum total of your shared dreams. The God who is able to do immeasurably more than all you can ask will accomplish something way beyond what you can imagine,[7] just as He did for David and his mighty men.

And remember, if your dream doesn't scare you, it's too small.

A DREAM WITHIN A DREAM

These are the names of David's mighty warriors.

2 Samuel 23:8

IN THE SUMMER OF 1896, twenty-five-year-old Orville Wright contracted typhoid fever. For several days he was in a near-death delirium. It would be an entire month before he could sit up in bed and several more weeks before he could get out of bed. And it may be the best thing that ever happened to him. Orville's brother, Wilbur, had taken an intense interest in human flight. And with Orville bedridden, he had a captive audience. Wilbur read aloud to Orville, and that's how the Wright brothers crossed paths with their lion.

Five-hundred-pound lions often hide within the pages of a book, just waiting for a dreamer to flip the page. Your dream may be one book, one page away.

Bishop Milton Wright had quite the library for the late nineteenth century. The bishop had a holy curiosity about all of life, but he had a particular fascination with the flight of birds, which explains an atypical title on his shelf, *Animal Mechanism: A Treatise on Terrestrial and Aerial Locomotion*. By the time Wilbur finished reading that book, he had discovered his destiny. The father's fascination had become the brothers' obsession.

On May 30, 1899, Wilbur wrote the most significant letter of his life, given the chain reaction it set in motion. He addressed the letter, written on Wright Cycle Company stationery, to the Smithsonian Institute, informing them that he had begun a systematic study of human flight. He asked for everything written on the subject, which wasn't much. But one book, *L'Empire de l'Air* by French farmer, poet, and student of flight Louis Pierre Mouillard, was like "a prophet crying in the wilderness, exhorting the world to repent of its unbelief in the possibility of human flight."[1]

Exhorting the world to repent of its unbelief in the possibility of human flight.

I like that sentence, a lot.

It convicts me, challenges me.

What impossibility do you need to repent of?

It's not just our sin that we need to repent of. It's our small dreams. The size of your dream may be the most accurate measure of the size of your God. Is He bigger than your biggest problem, your worst failure, your greatest mistake? Is He able to do immeasurably more than all you can ask or imagine?[2]

A God-sized dream will always be beyond your ability, beyond your resources. Unless God does it, it cannot be done! But that's how God gets the glory. If your dream doesn't scare you, it's too small. It also falls short of God's glory by not giving Him an opportunity to show up and show off His power.

This book is a call to repentance—*repent of your small dreams and your small God*. It's also a dare—*dare to go after a dream that is bigger than you are.*

To an infinite God, all finites are equal. There is no big or small, easy or difficult, possible or impossible. When Jesus walked out of the tomb on the third day, the word *impossible* was deleted from our dictionary. So quit focusing on the five-hundred-pound lion. Fix your eyes on the Lion of the tribe of Judah.

The impossible is an illusion.

The Wright brothers had no education, no crowd funding, and no friends in high places. All they had was a dream, but that's all it takes if it's coupled with tenacious stick-to-it-iveness. Over and over again, the Wright brothers failed to fly, but they refused to give up. They learned from each and every failure until they defied gravity for twelve seconds at Kitty Hawk, North Carolina, on December 17, 1903.

The impossible is temporary.

In the summer of 1896, human flight was science fiction. It's now our daily reality. At any given moment on any given day, five thousand airplanes carrying a million passengers are flying through the troposphere at three hundred miles per hour. And it all started with a dream. It always does. Wilbur Wright repented of his unbelief in the possibility of human flight, and the rest is history.

Don't just read this book.

Repent of unbelief in the possibility of your dream!

Inception

My wife, Lora, and I have a little tradition on Christmas Eve. We watch the 1946 classic *It's a Wonderful Life,* starring Jimmy Stewart. Our kids have a tradition too. They watch *Inception,* the science-fiction thriller written, directed, and produced by Christopher Nolan. It gets our kids into the Christmas spirit, I guess.

The plot line isn't easy to unravel, but extractors infiltrate the subconscious minds of their targets and extricate information while the targets are in a dream state. In one plot-changing scene, Dominic Cobb, played by Leonardo DiCaprio, goes beyond the art of extraction. He attempts the near-impossible task of inception—implanting an idea into a target's subconscious.

Cobb says to his partner in crime, Arthur, played by Joseph Gordon-Levitt, "We have to plant it deep in his subconscious." Arthur asks, "How deep?" Cobb says, "Three levels down." Arthur responds with a question that frames the film: "A dream within a dream within a dream—is that even possible?"[3]

Christopher Nolan's film popularized the phrase "a dream within a dream," but its etymology traces back to a poem by Edgar Allan Poe titled

"A Dream Within a Dream." The last stanza poses a question: "Is all that we see or seem but a dream within a dream?"[4]

The answer, I believe, is yes.

In the beginning God had a dream called creation. On the sixth day He created dreamers. That ability to imagine is unique to His image bearers.

Imagination is God's gift to you.

A dream is your gift back to God.

We assume that Adam and Eve would have remained in the Garden of Eden forever if they had not eaten from the tree of the knowledge of good and evil, but that is a misreading of the text. Long before Adam and Eve were banished from the garden, God told them to fill the earth and subdue it. It was a divine invitation to explore, to adventure, to discover, to dream.

Everything east of Eden was uncharted—196,949,970 square miles of virgin territory. Not unlike Christopher Columbus, who was commissioned by the king and queen of Spain to find a westward route to the Indies, or Lewis and Clark, who were commissioned by President Jefferson to explore the newly acquired Louisiana Territory, Adam and Eve were commissioned by God to subdue planet Earth.

The astronomer who charts the stars, the geneticist who maps the human genome, the researcher who seeks a cure for cancer, the developer who designs city centers, the oceanographer who explores the barrier reef, the ornithologist who studies rare bird species, the entrepreneur who starts businesses, the politician who drafts legislation, the physicist who chases quarks, and the chemist who charts molecular structures are all fulfilling the Genesis Commission in their own unique ways.

I don't know what dream God has given you, but it's a dream within a dream called *Creation*. It's also a story within a story called *Redemption*. God is writing His-story through you, and it always starts with a dream. You may not see yourself as a dreamer, but you are one. You have dreams that you aren't even aware of, dreams you haven't thought of as dreams. If you're a parent, for example, you have a dream. You even gave your dream a name when he or she was born.

Now let me narrow the aperture a little bit.

In the last days, God says,
>   I will pour out my Spirit on all people.
Your sons and daughters will prophesy,
>   your young men will see visions,
>   your old men will dream dreams.[5]

Dream dreams.

That's the natural, supernatural by-product of being filled with God's Spirit.

The Holy Spirit can and does perform inception. He implants dreams deep within the human spirit, three levels down. He also extracts dreams that have been dead and buried for decades, bringing them back to life. And He can do it in a thousand different ways.

For Wilbur Wright, it was a book he read at twenty-nine.

For me, it was a sermon I heard at nineteen.

For David, it was the day a prophet showed up on his doorstep.

The Dreamer

David was tending sheep just as he'd done the day before and the day before the day before. It's what he did; it's who he was. So when the prophet Samuel told David's father that one of his sons would become king, David's father didn't even bother to call David. Why? Because his earthly father didn't see David's potential. He saw a shepherd boy. Nothing more, nothing else.[6]

Samuel saw something else, something more.

As I look back on my dream journey, I'm eternally grateful for the prophets—coaches, teachers, pastors, mentors—who saw potential in me that I couldn't see in myself. At critical junctures they believed in me more than I believed in myself. Their words of encouragement gave me the courage to take steps of faith. Their words of wisdom helped me navigate difficult decisions. They are ordinary people with ordinary names—Don,

Bonnie, Bob, Karen, Bob, Bob, and Dick, just to name a few. Like Samuel with David, they helped me discover my destiny.

You never know when or where or how destiny will knock on your door, but it rarely has a scheduled appointment. More often than not, you don't discover your dream. Your dream discovers you when you are faithfully tending sheep.

David was a giant killer, a songwriter, and the king of Israel. But before he was any of those things, David was a dreamer. Samuel did more than anoint David's head; he implanted a dream in David's heart. And like any God-sized dream, it would take time and it would take a team.

The Dream Team

Second Samuel 23 is more than a laundry list of thirty-seven names. It's a who's who list. In the pages that follow, I'll detail some of their heroic deeds. These were David's best friends, his closest confidants. Not only was their courage unmatched, but their loyalty to David was undivided. To a man, they were ready to trade their lives for David's life. And that raises a few questions: What drew these mighty men to David? Why would they cast lots with a fugitive? What turned these ragtag rebels into a band of brothers who would risk their lives for what seemed like a lost cause?

The mighty men were drawn to a dreamer with a God-sized dream. And that's what will draw people to you.

Without his band of brothers, David's dream of becoming king was a pipe dream. His destiny was tied to theirs, and their destiny was tied to his. David's dream became their dream, a dream within a dream.

Our dreams are more intricately interwoven across time and space than any of us could ever imagine. Your dreams are possible because of the dreams that were dreamed before you. And the domino effect of your dreams will be felt for generations.

Benaiah helped David fulfill his destiny, and David became the king of Israel. But it was a two-way street. David helped Benaiah's dreams come true too. When the crown was passed from David to his son Solomon forty years later, Benaiah was promoted from bodyguard to commander in chief of Israel's army. And the same was true of Solomon. It was David's dream that set up Solomon as king of Israel, but it was Solomon who fulfilled his father's dream of building a temple in Jerusalem.

Your greatest legacy isn't your dream. Your greatest legacy is the next generation of dreamers that your dream inspires—the dreams within a dream.

One of my dreams is to pastor one church for life, and I've been living the dream for the last twenty years. But it's really a dream within a dream. My father-in-law, Bob Schmidgall, planted and pastored Calvary Church in Naperville, Illinois, for thirty-one years. I had a front-row seat to watch long obedience in the same direction. I saw what God could do if you plant yourself in one place and let your roots grow deep. His dream implanted a seed in my spirit, three levels down.

My dream isn't my legacy.

My dream is my father-in-law's legacy.

My dream wasn't birthed on January 7, 1996, the day I started pastoring a core group of nineteen people called National Community Church. My dream within a dream was conceived in July of 1967 when my father-in-law started Calvary Church.

Our dreams predate us.

They were born long before we were.

Our dreams postdate us.

They make a difference long after we are gone.

The Dreamcatcher

Our extended family gathered around the fireplace this past Thanksgiving and listened to a sermon my father-in-law preached on February 21, 1979. He died eighteen years ago, so some of his grandchildren had never heard his voice.

It was an amazing message on vision, but one preliminary comment caught my attention. My father-in-law honored E. M. Clark, who was in the audience that day. He referred to Clark, the district superintendent of the Illinois Assemblies of God, as a spiritual father.

I never met E. M. Clark. And until hearing that sermon, I had no idea that he had such a profound impact on my father-in-law's life. But I'm the secondary beneficiary. If E. M. Clark was my father-in-law's spiritual father, that makes me his spiritual grandson.

E. M. Clark was a dreamcatcher. His dream was leveraging other people's dreams, and it's evidenced by his motto that became the mantra of the Illinois district: "Come share your dream with us, and let us help you fulfill it."

In the mid-1960s two young dreamers named Bob Schmidgall and Dick Foth responded to that clarion call. Dick and Ruth Foth planted a church near the University of Illinois in Urbana. Bob and Karen Schmidgall planted a church in Naperville, Illinois. They were the young guns of the Illinois district, and both churches followed a similar growth curve during their first decade. Dick Foth left the pastorate to become the president of Bethany College in Santa Cruz, California, but Dick and Bob remained close friends across the country, across the years.

Now let me connect the dots.

Right before Lora and I chased a lion to Washington, DC, in 1994, Dick and Ruth Foth relocated to the nation's capital to work behind the scenes with the who's who of Washington in embassies, at the Pentagon, and in the halls of Congress.

The Foths not only invited Lora and me over for dinner our first Thanksgiving in DC, but they treated us like family. In fact, Dick Foth has been my spiritual father for the past twenty years. His influence on my life is incalculable.

Twenty years ago when nineteen people showed up for our first service, two of them were Dick and Ruth Foth. And they invited their friends Senator John and Janet Ashcroft. They not only gave us much-needed moral support, but they also gave the lion's share of financial support since our core group consisted primarily of college students.

If you do the math, 21 percent of our core group was the direct result of a friendship that my father-in-law had cultivated with Dick Foth before I was even born. And that friendship was the by-product of a dreamcatcher who said, "Come share your dream with us, and we'll help you fulfill it."

My point? My dream is a dream within a dream within a dream. And so is yours. Your dream has a genealogy. Honor your upline! Your dream also has progeny. Empower your downline! And remember, your life is one subplot in God's grand narrative—the story arc of redemption.

One footnote: your legacy isn't just your God-sized dreams.

It's also your small acts of kindness.

E. M. Clark was a spiritual father to my father-in-law, but he did more than just help him fulfill his dream. One act of kindness made all the difference in the world. During the early days of their dream journey, a dozen college students spent a summer in Naperville, Illinois, helping my in-laws plant Calvary Church. E. M. and his wife, Estella, visited one weekend, and my mother-in-law served them hot dogs, chips, and Kool-Aid. That's all she and my father-in-law could afford. On the way out of town, the Clarks stopped at the grocery store and bought steaks, baked potatoes, and ice cream for the entire team. A few days later my mother-in-law received a gift in the mail—an electric knife, which she still uses forty-nine years later! It's the gift that keeps on giving. Not just the knife, but also the dream.

Dream Inventory

When I inventory my dreams, I realize that all of them are a dream within a dream. The dream of writing a book about Benaiah was inspired by a sermon I heard when I was nineteen years old. So that book is really a dream within a sermon by Sam Farina. The dream of creating a family foundation was inspired by Jim Linen and the Des Plaines Charitable Trust, where I've had the privilege of serving as a trustee for the past decade. Even our dream of meeting in movie theaters at metro stops is a dream within a dream. The idea was implanted in my subconscious as I listened to the history of Willow Creek Community Church at one of their leadership conferences.

This year we opened a first-rate, second-run movie theater on Capitol

Hill. It's an expression of our core conviction: *the church belongs in the middle of the marketplace.* In my opinion filmmakers are postmodern prophets, and movie screens are postmodern stained glass.

Too often the church complains about culture instead of creating it. The energy we spend on criticism is being stolen from creativity. It's sideways energy. We need fewer commentators and more innovators. I try to live by Michelangelo's maxim: *criticize by creating.* Quit complaining about what's wrong, and do something that makes a difference!

Write a better book.

Start a better business.

Create a better product.

Run a better campaign.

Draft a better bill.

Produce a better movie.

In the 1930s a producer at 20th Century Fox wrote a letter to presidents of several prominent Christian colleges, asking them to send him screenwriters. His dream was to produce films with a redemptive subplot. One president wrote back and said he'd sooner send his young people to hell itself than send them to Hollywood.[7]

What a missed opportunity!

Now let me get off my soapbox and make my point. A church opening a movie theater is a little out of the box, but even that dream is a dream within a dream.

In 1960 an evangelist named R. W. Schambach was holding a revival in Washington, DC. As he walked by a movie theater at 535 Eighth Street SE, he felt prompted to pray that God would shut down the theater and turn it into a church. Two years later it became the People's Church. And forty-nine years later it would become National Community Church.

I'll never forget our first gathering. We packed the place—not just the sanctuary and the lobby. We had people spilling onto the sidewalk. Michael Hall, the pastor of the People's Church, was there that night.

Afterward, Michael said, "Mark, many years ago I had a vision, and in that vision our church was packed with young people raising their hands in worship. The church was so full that I saw people worshiping God out the front door and onto the sidewalk." Michael had dreamed that dream for a long time, and it became reality that night. "I thought the vision was for me," he said. "But now I realize it was for you."

I'm eternally grateful to our dear friends Michael and Terry Hall. It took tremendous courage for the People's Church to sell us their building, and the prayers they prayed in that place for forty-nine years are still being answered. Everything God does in and through National Community Church is a prayer within a prayer. We are reaping where we have not sown.

Along with having our four weekend gatherings, we decided to turn our Capitol Hill campus back into an art-deco theater where the church and community could cross paths. We recently hung a blade sign outside the theater. We decided to name it what it was—*The Miracle*. It's also a way of honoring R. W. Schambach, whose fifty-six-year-old prayer made it possible.

In the wake of his revivals, Schambach would sometimes start a church. The first one was in Newark, New Jersey, in 1959. He also started churches in Philadelphia, Chicago, and Brooklyn. Each one was given the same name—Miracle Temple. We dropped "Temple" and added "Theatre." But it's a testimony to a dreamer—a name within a name, a prayer within a prayer, a dream within a dream.

The story God is writing through your life is someone else's subplot.

It was true for David's mighty men.

It's true for me.

And it's true for you.

THE RIPPLE EFFECT

In one encounter

2 Samuel 23:8

PAUL TUDOR JONES IS A Wall Street legend.

The founder of the Tudor Investment Corporation made his mark on Black Monday, October 19, 1987. It still ranks as the largest one-day percentage drop of the Dow Jones Industrial Average, yet Jones managed to triple his investment value by shorting his portfolio. And he's no one-hit wonder. Jones has defied financial gravity ever since, earning positive returns for twenty-eight consecutive years. As a contrarian, he looks for opportunities where others see red flags. When investors bail out on a bear market, he goes bear hunting. And he's not afraid of grabbing a bull market by the horns and taking a wild ride.[1]

Paul Tudor Jones lives by a few market maxims: *always have a mental stop, never average losers,* and *let go of mistakes you made three seconds ago.* But his investment philosophy is epitomized by one guiding principle: *stay in the game for as long as you can.* Few people play the investment game better than Jones, but becoming a billionaire wasn't the five-hundred-pound lion he was chasing. Jones set his sights much higher than that.

In 1986 Jones adopted a sixth-grade class at an underperforming public school in New York City. Despite his guaranteeing a college scholarship to every high school graduate, only one-third of those kids got their high school diplomas. Jones admittedly had underestimated the environmental challenges that inner-city kids face, but that failure fueled his passion to fight poverty. Instead of giving up the fight, Jones started the Robin Hood

Foundation. Since its inception in 1988, Robin Hood has channeled $1.45 billion to the cause Jones cares so deeply about. It's also inspired other venture philanthropists. *Fortune* magazine has called the Robin Hood Foundation "one of the most innovative and influential philanthropic organizations of our time."[2]

Paul Tudor Jones is as competitive as they come, evidenced by the welterweight boxing championship he won in his twenties. He's a fighter. But like the warrior-poet David, he has another side to his personality. The driving engine of his life is one act of kindness. When he was a child, Jones was at an outdoor vegetable market with his mother one day and got lost.

> When you're four years old, your mother is everything. And this extraordinarily kind, very old, very tall black man came over and said, "Don't worry. We're going to find your momma. Don't cry, we're going to find her. You're going to be happy in a minute."
>
> You never forget stuff like that. God's every action, those little actions become so much bigger, and then they become multiplicative. We forget how important the smallest action can be. For me, I think, it kind of spawned a lifetime of trying to always repay that kindness.[3]

What was the name of that very old, very tall black man? I have no idea, and neither does Paul Tudor Jones. And he's probably been dead for quite some time. But that one act of kindness inspired a lifetime of philanthropy! Paul Tudor Jones may have founded the Robin Hood Foundation, but it was a complete stranger who provided the inspiration. Every grant the foundation gives is a gift within a gift.

"In one encounter."

That little phrase in 2 Samuel 23 is so simple yet so powerful. That's all it takes! You are one encounter away from your destiny. One off-the-cuff conversation, one crazy idea, or one glance across a crowded room can change everything.

What's true for Josheb-Basshebeth is true for you. Just like the highest-ranking member of David's mighty men, you might need to make a move.

Epic Challenges

A few years ago I spent two formative days in New York City with screen-writing sage Robert McKee. His Story Seminar is like a postgraduate education in storytelling. We dissected text and subtext, story and backstory, setup and payoff, beat and arc, conflict and resolution.

I originally signed up for the seminar because I thought I might want to try my hand at screenwriting, but the process totally reframed the way I see my own storyline. One overarching observation was a game changer: *No conflict. No story.*

We accept that fact when it comes to movies. Epic movies demand epic conflict. That's what makes them epic! And what's true of great movies is true of great lives. Great conflict cultivates great character. Of course, it's easier to watch on the screen than it is to walk through it.

If you want to live an epic life, you have to overcome some epic challenges. You have to take some epic risks, make some epic sacrifices.

For David it was picking a fight with Goliath.

For Benaiah it was chasing the lion.

For Josheb it was taking his stand when the rest of the army retreated.

In every storyline there are defining moments. The technical term, in terms of plot structure, is "inciting incident." It's a turning point, a tipping point. It's a point of no return.

Inciting incidents come in two basic varieties: things that happen to you that you cannot control and things you make happen that you can control. Of course, even if something is out of your control, you still control your reaction. You might not be responsible, but you are response-able. And it's the ability to choose your response that will likely determine your destiny.

Some inciting incidents are perceived as positive, like a college scholarship or a job promotion. Others are perceived as negative, like a pink slip or a positive diagnosis. But don't be too quick to judge a blessing or a curse by its cover. What we perceive as positive sometimes turns out to have negative side effects, and what we perceive as negative often turns out to be the best thing that ever happened to us.

After an unsuccessful attempt at church planting in Chicago, I felt like a complete failure. But if that church plant had succeeded, we never would have made the move to Washington, DC. So in hindsight, that failure was one of the best things that ever happened to me.

Mismanaged success is the leading cause of failure.

Well-managed failure is the leading cause of success.

I haven't won the war with pride—it's a daily battle. But failure is one key to winning that war. It shows us what we're capable of, and in my case it's not much! Without God's help, I'm below average. That failed church plant taught me an invaluable lesson: unless the Lord builds the house, we labor in vain.[4] Of course, the flip side is true too. If God builds it, nothing can hinder it.

I've pastored National Community Church in Washington, DC, for two decades now. We've had the privilege of touching tens of thousands of lives, and the best is yet to come. It's hard to imagine what our lives would be like if we hadn't taken that step of faith and moved to Washington, DC. We would have forfeited so many blessings. But like every dream journey, it traces back to an inciting incident—a 595-mile step of faith from Chicago to DC. We had no place to live and no guaranteed salary when we packed all our belongings into a fifteen-foot U-Haul truck, but we knew God was calling us.

What do you need to do to make your dream happen? Maybe it's taking that first step of faith or burning some bridges behind you. After all, you can't steal second base if you keep your foot on first. Maybe it's taking response-ability for something that has handicapped you for far too long. The one thing I'm certain of is this: it'll take some two-o'clock-in-the-morning courage!

The Ripple Effect

Inciting incidents come in lots of sizes, shapes, and colors. Some are as bold and brash as Benaiah chasing a lion. Others are as subtle and gentle as the act of kindness that influenced Paul Tudor Jones. But either way, never underestimate the power of one act of kindness, one act of courage, one act of generosity.

The Battle of Jericho ranks as one of the most significant turning points in the Jewish storyline. It was the first victory in the Promised Land, but the key to victory was an act of kindness. And that act of kindness is the key to your salvation.

When the Israelites sent two spies into Jericho to do reconnaissance, they were nearly captured. It was a prostitute named Rahab who saved their lives by risking hers. Harboring Jewish spies was akin to treason. So before helping them escape, Rahab cut a deal. She simply asked them to return the favor: "Please swear to me by the Lord that you will show kindness to my family, because I have shown kindness to you."[5]

Rahab was thinking exclusively of her immediate family. It was a present-tense request, but it had future-tense ramifications. By showing kindness to Rahab, those Jewish spies were also showing kindness to her great-great-grandson David. That one act of kindness had a ripple effect across nations and generations.

According to rabbinic tradition, Rahab was one of the four most beautiful women in Scripture. The other three were Sarai, Abigail, and Esther. And according to tradition, Rahab converted to Judaism at the age of fifty. She fell in love with Salmon, a Jewish man from the tribe of Judah. They had a son named Boaz, who had a son named Obed, who had a son named Jesse, who had a son named David.

You never know whom you are showing kindness to. It might be the great-great-grandmother of a king. It might be a future billionaire who will become a venture philanthropist. Or it might be your future son-in-law.

When I was thirteen years old, I was in the intensive care unit at Edward Hospital in Naperville, Illinois. Around two o'clock in the morning, I felt as if I was taking my final breath. The doctors called code blue, and my parents called our pastor, Bob Schmidgall. We had just started going to the church he pastored, and it was a church of thousands, so he didn't even know us. But that didn't keep him from coming to the hospital in the middle of the night to pray for me. He didn't know it at the time, but he was praying for his future son-in-law. I married his daughter nine years later, and we gave him his first grandchild.

Sometimes the seeds of our dreams don't germinate for months or years or decades. But if we plant and water, God will give the increase in due time. Why? Because you cannot break the law of sowing and reaping. It will make or break you.

> Let us not become weary in doing good, for at the proper time
> we will reap a harvest if we do not give up. Therefore, as we have
> opportunity, let us do good to all people.[6]

When it comes to the ripple effect, Rahab is exhibit A.

She wasn't just King David's great-great-grandmother. She's also listed in the genealogy of Jesus. It might sound like a stretch, but one act of kindness had something to do with your salvation. If Rahab hadn't saved the lives of the spies, and if the spies hadn't saved the life of Rahab, she would have missed the opportunity to be part of the line and lineage of Jesus. That line and lineage would have been cut off eighteen generations before His birth in Bethlehem.

You're a secondary beneficiary of that act of kindness!

One Raspberry

On September 3, 1939, German troops invaded Bielsko, Poland. A fifteen-year-old girl, Gerda Weissman, and her family survived in a Jewish ghetto until June of 1942. That's when Gerda was torn from her mother. Her mother, Helene, was sent to a death camp. Gerda would spend three years in a Nazi concentration camp, followed by a 350-mile death march that she somehow survived. By the time she was liberated by American troops, Gerda was a sixty-eight-pound skeleton. And in what must rank as one of the most improbable love stories ever, Gerda actually married the soldier who found her, Lieutenant Kurt Klein.[7]

There are six glass towers at the Holocaust Memorial in Boston, Massachusetts, representing the six extermination camps where six million Jews lost their lives. Five towers tell the story of unconscionable cruelty and unimaginable suffering, but the sixth tower stands as a testimony to hope. Inscribed on it is a short story titled "One Raspberry," written by Gerda Weissman Klein.

> Ilse, a childhood friend of mine, once found a raspberry in the camp and carried it in her pocket all day to present to me that night on a leaf. Imagine a world in which your entire possession is one raspberry and you gave it to your friend.[8]

The true measure of a gift is what you gave up to give it. One raspberry isn't much unless it's all you have! Then it's not next to nothing; it's everything. The same is true of two billion dollars or two mites. Big dreams often start with small acts of kindness. It's powerful when we're on the receiving end, but it's even more wonderful when we're on the giving end.

Every act of kindness creates a ripple effect. When you make someone's day, you don't just make his or her day, because there's a good chance that he or she will make someone else's day. Where the ripple effect of kindness ends, no one knows. And the same is true of love and grace and courage. Give it a generation or two or eighteen, and it might just be the inciting incident that changes the course of history.

Inciting Incidents

Most of us don't run billion-dollar foundations like Paul Tudor Jones or aid and abet international spies like Rahab, so let me bring this idea down to earth. Some inciting incidents are obvious, like renting a U-Haul and moving to Washington, DC. But many inciting incidents fly under the radar of our consciousness. We don't realize the impact they had on us until many years later.

One of my earliest memories is a four-year-old friend telling me I couldn't ride his bike anymore because his dad had taken off the training wheels. After making his proclamation, he rode his bike back to his house three doors down. I immediately marched down to his house, pedaled his bike back to my house, and triumphantly kicked down the kickstand in my driveway.

If you want me to do something, don't tell me to *do it*. That's not motivating to me. Tell me *it can't be done*. That's the way I'm wired. I have this subliminal, and sometimes unsanctified, impulse to prove prognosticators wrong. I'm drawn to overwhelming odds, impossible challenges.

Another one of my inciting incidents is a movie called *The Hiding Place*, a Billy Graham film about another Holocaust survivor named Corrie ten Boom. I was only five years old when I saw it, which makes me wonder why my parents took me. But that film was the beginning of my faith journey. Is it any coincidence that I pastor a multisite church that meets in movie theaters and produces trailers for its sermon series? Is it any coincidence that one of my life goals is to produce a film? We try to influence others the way we were influenced. For me it was a film. And where that ripple effect ends, only God knows.

One of the best ways to discover your destiny is to study your history. The seeds of your dreams are often buried in your memory, three levels down.

Take inventory.

Subliminal Messages

Some of my earliest memories are of sitting in services at Trinity Covenant Church in Crystal, Minnesota. The order of service was printed on the bulletin every week, and I distinctly remember checking them off one by one with the pew pencil. Honestly, I was bored stiff by church. Of course, I was also six years old. One way I entertained myself was by filling out offering envelopes and dropping them in the plate as it passed by. Trinity Covenant got quite a few multimillion-dollar gifts from superheroes with childlike handwriting.

My most memorable church service was the day my dad picked up a pack of Topps football cards and let me open them during church. Revival almost broke out when I got two Vikings receivers, Ahmad Rashad and Sammy White.

Those memories may seem like minor incidents in my ancient past, but they were inciting incidents. As a pastor, I have a subliminal fear of people just checking off an order of service. I believe church should be anything but boring! When people miss church they should actually *miss* church.

Did you know that your eye makes tiny movements called micro-saccades almost constantly? They are the fastest movements executed by the human body, so fast that they can be observed only with special instrumentation. The six muscles controlling your eyeball twitch about a hundred thousand times each day![9]

In much the same way, there are a hundred thousand subliminal motivations that control our everyday movements. They operate below the level of consciousness, but they dictate why we do what we do more than we are aware of.

In the second grade you excitedly raised your hand, only to give the wrong answer. Thirty years later you hesitate to interject your ideas in the boardroom because your classmates laughed at you and you're afraid of the same thing happening again. Or flip the script. You have measured confidence in critical situations because you hit a game-winning free throw in junior high. Big or small, good or bad, a handful of experiences influence the way we see ourselves, the way we see life. It's not until we inventory our inciting incidents that we begin to see why we do what we do.

Here's what I'm sure of. If you've overcome eight-hundred-to-one odds, like Josheb, not much overwhelms you after that. If you've chased a lion into a pit on a snowy day, like Benaiah, not much scares you after that. If you've defeated a Philistine giant on the field of battle, like David, not much intimidates you after that.

You have to inventory God's faithfulness so you can draw faith from those past successes, past miracles, past blessings. And the good news is that God's faithfulness cannot be overdrawn!

Better Stories

I was first introduced to the idea of inciting incidents in Donald Miller's brilliant book *A Million Miles in a Thousand Years*. In fact, that's what inspired me to take Robert McKee's Story Seminar. As an offshoot of that book, Don started a company called Storyline, and I love its mission: to help people tell better stories with their lives.

Are you living your life in a way that is worth telling stories about?

When Don spoke at National Community Church a few years ago, he shared one of his inciting incidents. Don is a *New York Times* best-selling author who has sold millions of books, but during his younger years he was somewhat of a misfit. Actually, his self-assessment is a little more brutal: "I wasn't good at anything."

Then Don was asked to write a short article for his high school youth group newsletter. That's when one unscripted encounter, one compliment rewrote his storyline. Someone said, "Don, you're a really good writer."

It was the first time anyone had told Don he was good at anything.

That punch line punctuates Don's life. It put a period on his feelings of incompetence and began a new sentence, a new chapter in his life.

God wants to write His story through your life. And if you give Him complete editorial control, He'll write an epic. Of course, it'll involve some epic conflict. But the God who began a good work in you will carry it to completion, even if it takes eighteen generations!

Telling a better story with your life begins with identifying the inciting incidents in your past. That's your backstory. Then you start creating incidents with intentionality. That's the rest of the story.

THE DOOR TO THE FUTURE

He raised his spear against eight hundred men.

2 Samuel 23:8

WILSON BENTLEY WAS BORN and raised on a farm in Jericho, Vermont. As a young boy he developed a fascination for snowflakes. Most people seek shelter during snowstorms, but not Wilson. He would run outside when the flakes started falling, catch them on black velvet, look at them under a microscope, and take photographs of them before they melted. His first photomicrograph of a snowflake was taken on January 15, 1885.

> Under the microscope, I found that snowflakes were miracles of beauty; and it seemed a shame that this beauty should not be seen and appreciated by others. Every crystal was a masterpiece of design and no one design was ever repeated. When a snowflake melted, that design was forever lost. Just that much beauty was gone, without leaving any record behind.[1]

Wilson Bentley chased his dream for more than half a century, amassing 5,381 photographs that were published in his magnum opus, *Snow Crystals*. Then Wilson died a fitting death, a death that epitomized his life. Wilson "Snowflake" Bentley contracted pneumonia after walking six miles through a snowstorm and died on December 23, 1931.

I want to die that way! No, not from pneumonia. I want to die doing what I love to do, doing what God has called me to do. I want to pursue God-sized dreams until the day I die. And if it kills me, so be it. What a way to go!

I'm not convinced that our true date of death is the date listed on our death certificate. Sadly, many people die long before their heart stops beating. We start dying the day we stop dreaming. And ironically, we start living the day we discover a dream worth dying for.

That's what the mighty men found in David—a cause worth living for, a dream worth dying for. If you don't have a dream, get around people who do. You might just catch what they have. Dreams are highly contagious!

We know very little about Josheb-Basshebeth. He gets only one sentence of sacred text. But at some point, Josheb stopped lifting weights and started lifting his spear in David's defense. It was no longer about going to the gym and admiring himself in the mirror. By the way, if you're a gym rat, make sure it's not a one-way mirror! I have a friend, one of our campus pastors, who flexed in front of a mirror for about five minutes, not realizing that a yoga class on the other side was watching the whole thing. I won't mention his initials, but his name is Dave Schmidgall. They even clapped for him when he finished flexing!

Don't read this the wrong way. I'm all for gym memberships. And the mighty men were *mighty*. But in my experience, working out for the sake of working out is demotivating. We need a goal to go after, like running a marathon or dropping two waist sizes. That's when our workouts take on a new dimension of motivation.

I need a life goal to keep me going.

I need a noble cause to keep me committed.

I need a God-sized dream to keep me from getting demotivated.

We don't die when our hearts stop beating. We die when our hearts stop skipping a beat in pursuit of our passions, when our hearts stop breaking for the things that break the heart of God.

One Verse

If you reverse-engineer the history of time, every atom in the universe can trace its origin back to the four words by which God spoke everything into existence: "Let there be light." According to the Doppler effect, those four words are still creating galaxies at the outer edges of the universe.

In much the same way, there are genesis moments in every dream journey. A dream is implanted in your spirit by the Spirit of God, and the rest of your life is the ripple effect. It changes the plot line of your life forever.

For Wilson Bentley the genesis moment was the day his schoolteacher mother gave him a microscope. Wilson loved observing anything and everything under the scope. But growing up in the Snowbelt, with an average annual snowfall of 120 inches, he developed a special fondness for snowflakes.

At age sixteen Wilson learned about a camera that could be coupled with a microscope to take pictures. It took a year of savings to buy the camera. It took another year of failed attempts to capture his first photograph. What kept him going after each failed attempt? One verse of Scripture, Job 38:22: "Have you entered the storehouses of the snow?"

This is one of fifty-one unanswerable questions that God asked during his pop quiz of Job.[2] We read them as rebukes, and they are. The Omniscient One was putting Job in his intellectual place. But I also see them as leading questions, questions that summon us to scientific inquiry. It even says, "Stop and consider God's wonders."[3] That's precisely what Wilson Bentley was doing with each photomicrograph of a snowflake.

Wilson Bentley devoted his life to answering that one question, exploring the meaning of that one verse of Scripture. That one verse was the driving motivation of Bentley's life. And his life became its interpretation. As one biographer noted, "The Great Designer found an interpreter in an insignificant country boy."[4]

I've already shared this theory, but it's worth sharing again: over time your favorite scripture becomes the script of your life. The promises of God become the plot line of your life. And the more you rehearse those lines, the more you get into character—the character of Christ. Your life becomes a unique interpretation of that life verse.

For Wilson Bentley it was Job 38:22.

For me it's 2 Samuel 23:20.

What verse is your life exegeting, interpreting, translating?

Page 23

I recently had the privilege of speaking at Brooklyn Tabernacle. It's famous for its choir, which has won six Grammys. But what's impressive to me is the three thousand people who show up for their prayer meeting on Tuesday nights.

In the late 1800s, Brooklyn Tab had a six-thousand-seat church building. Over the subsequent century, the church gradually dwindled until thirty people were left. That's when Jim Cymbala became pastor.

Jim was trying to turn the ship, but nothing he tried was working. "We couldn't finesse it," Jim said. "We couldn't organize, market and program our way out." That's when Jim got a revelation from God on a fishing boat off the coast of Florida:

> If you and your wife will lead My people to pray and call upon
> My name, you will never lack for something fresh to preach. I will
> supply all the money that's needed . . . and you will never have a
> building large enough to contain the crowds I will send.[5]

God threw down the gauntlet, and Jim raised his spear!

It was a genesis moment for Jim and for Brooklyn Tab. He bet all his marbles on God's promise in 2 Chronicles 7:14, and God has delivered. If you ever visit Brooklyn Tab, you better get there early. And that's just to get a seat in the overflow room!

One footnote.

My friend Steven Furtick is a powerful preacher and a visionary leader. What was the genesis moment in his dream journey? Page 23 of Jim Cymbala's book *Fresh Wind, Fresh Fire,* where it says, "I despaired at the thought that my life might slip by without seeing God show himself mightily on our behalf." That one statement jumped off the page and into Steven's spirit. Steven calls it his page 23 vision.[6]

My point? Steven's vision for Elevation Church is a dream within a dream! Jim is Steven's upline, and Steven is Jim's downline. And I'm praying that God gives you a page 23 vision as you read *Chase the Lion*. If He does, leaf the page! It's the beginning of a new chapter in your life.

Genesis Moments

English novelist Graham Greene ranks as one of the greatest writers of the twentieth century. His sixty-seven-year writing career produced twenty-five novels. His life's work was crafting storylines, which adds credence to my favorite sentence of his: "There is always one moment in childhood when the door opens and lets the future in."[7]

What's true in fiction is true in life.

There are genesis moments in every dream journey that radically change the plot line of our lives. It's impossible to predict when or where or how they will occur. But once the door to the future opens, the door to the past slams shut. There is no turning back.

It's a new day, a new normal.

One verse. One decision. One risk. One idea.

That's all it takes.

The door to the future opened for me in a high school speech class. I gave a speech that doubled as my first sermon. I'm not sure any of my classmates had a revelation, but it was a genesis moment in my storyline. I've preached a thousand sermons since then, but that was the first.

Unbeknownst to me, my mom gave a copy of that speech to my grandma, who gave a copy to her Bible study teacher. That Bible study teacher, whom I never even met, gave it higher marks than my speech teacher! He asked my grandma, "Has Mark ever thought about ministry?"

At that point in my storyline, the answer was no. I hadn't given ministry a single thought. But when that compliment was relayed from my grandma to my mom to me, it implanted a seed in my spirit, three levels down.

Don't underestimate the power of one compliment.

One word of encouragement has the potential to change a person's perspective on life, a person's plot line for all eternity. And don't just compliment people to their faces. Brag about them behind their backs! The right word at the right time can be the catalyst for someone else's dream.

There is always a moment when the door opens—a genesis moment when God reveals Himself in a burning bush on the backside of the desert, a genesis moment when God knocks you off your horse on the road to Damascus, a genesis moment when God shows off His power at Pentecost.

For David the genesis moment was the day a prophet showed up unannounced on his family's front doorstep.

For Benaiah it was chasing a lion into a pit on a snowy day. That split-second decision opened the door to the future—a job as King David's bodyguard. And that door opened another door—commander in chief of Israel's army.

For Josheb-Basshebeth it was raising his spear against eight hundred of David's sworn enemies. That one act of two-o'clock-in-the-morning courage opened the door and earned him a seat of honor at David's round table. Not one of David's mighty men outranked Josheb.

Impossible Odds

"May the odds be ever in your favor."

That is the motto of the Hunger Games, but that isn't how it works in the kingdom of God. It's more like "May the odds be ever against you." Impossible odds set the stage for God's greatest miracles! And apparently God loves long shots.

Isn't that why He removed 9,700 soldiers from Gideon's army?

Isn't that why He let the fiery furnace be heated seven times hotter?

Isn't that why He didn't show up until Lazarus was four days dead?

If the Israelites had defeated the Midianites with an army of 10,000, I'm sure they would have thanked God. But I bet they would have taken some of the credit themselves. So God cut the army down to size. He let Nebuchadnezzar turn up the heat. He let Lazarus lie in a tomb for four days. Why? To ensure He got all the credit, all the glory.

We tend to avoid situations where the odds are against us, but when we do, we rob God of the opportunity to do something supernatural.

We read right past it, but Josheb raised his spear against 800. If you want to appreciate how many people that is, try singing "800 Philistine soldiers in the field, 800 Philistine soldiers. Take one down, do it again, 799 Philistine soldiers in the field."

Those are some long odds! But that's how one man became chief of David's mighty men. He beat 800-to-1 odds!

When was the last time you attempted something that was destined to fail without divine intervention?

When National Community Church was just a year old, we gave away fifty thousand pounds of groceries to five thousand guests at our first Convoy of Hope outreach. We knew we needed four hundred volunteers to pull it off, and our average attendance was less than a hundred people. We were in way over our heads, but several area churches rallied around us, and a thousand people crossed the line of faith! It was a banner day! Why? Because we raised our swords, even when the odds were against us.

Just when I think I'm dreaming big, God often does something that reveals how small my dream is in comparison to His omnipotence. In the past decade God has performed one real-estate miracle after another for NCC. We've acquired half a dozen properties despite the fact that property goes for about $14 million an acre in our neck of the woods. The latest miracle was a $29.3 million castle on Capitol Hill. I didn't have a category for a city block, and I certainly didn't have a category for the price tag! Plus, we were up against an investment firm that offered cash. It felt like 800-to-1 odds!

The odds were not in our favor, but that's how God gets more glory.

The Genesis Question

Brian Grazer is an accomplished film producer with forty-three Academy Award nominations to his credit. I like many of Brian's movies, but I love his approach to life even more. He revealed one secret to his success in his book, *A Curious Mind*. For decades Brian has had what he calls "curiosity conversations" with successful people, ranging from scientists to spies. "Life isn't about finding the answers," Brian said. "It's about asking the questions."[8]

Like Brian, I love questioning people about their dream journeys. And my favorite question is what I call "the genesis question." Even more than stories, I love backstories. So I ask this question: What was the genesis of your dream?

The first time I asked the genesis question was at a dinner with pastor and author Rick Warren. There were twenty-five of us, sitting at multiple tables, so I didn't want to monopolize Rick's time. But as a new author I wanted to hear about the genesis of his runaway bestseller, *The Purpose Driven Life*.

Before Rick was offered a contract to write that book, Saddleback Church initiated a building campaign. As the pastor of the church, Rick wanted to set the standard, so he and his wife, Kay, pledged the equivalent of three years of his salary to the campaign. Shortly after making that pledge, Rick signed a two-book deal for *The Purpose Driven Church* and *The Purpose Driven Life*.

The advance was the same dollar amount as the pledge!

Coincidence? I think not. And considering that *The Purpose Driven Life* is one of the best-selling nonfiction books of all time, I dare say Rick has recouped his advance. Knowing that backstory made me respect Rick all the more.

How has *The Purpose Driven Life* become one of the best-selling non-fiction books in history? Well, how readers will respond to a book is a bit of a mystery, as every author knows. *The Purpose Driven Life* certainly hit a nerve ending, a deep-seated desire for purpose. But here's my take: God has honored Rick's books because Rick honored God with a pledge. That three-year pledge was a genesis moment. And for the record, every act of generosity is! If you want God to do something beyond your ability, try giving beyond your means. It's a great starting point, a leverage point.

On a much smaller scale, I believe that God has honored *In a Pit with a Lion on a Snowy Day* because of a $5,000 pledge my wife and I made to missions on July 31, 2005. That faith promise didn't fit in our budget, but we believed that God would somehow provide what we promised. Sixty-five days later I signed my first book contract.

The book deal was a dream come true, but so was writing a $5,000 check to missions! And I believe it was our pledge that made the writing dream come true.

It was our way of raising the spear like Josheb.

It was our way of chasing the lion like Benaiah.

Every God-sized dream has a genesis—a God-ordained opportunity, a God-given passion. But at some point you need to raise your spear of faith. That's how the door opens and lets the future in.

What spear do you need to raise?

What odds do you need to defy?

What verse do you need to interpret with your life?

THE GAME OF INCHES

He was with David when they taunted the Philistines.

2 Samuel 23:9

IN THE SUMMER OF 1957, twelve-year-old Ed Catmull was driving cross-country with his family to Yellowstone National Park. As they zigzagged on a canyon road with no guardrail, a car driving in the opposite direction drifted into their lane. Ed remembers his mom screaming, his dad swerving. They came within two inches of driving off the cliff, game over.

That's how close we came to missing *Finding Nemo*, *The Incredibles*, and *Up*. Why? Because Ed Catmull is the founder and president of Pixar Animation Studios. So as I see it, no Ed means no *Toy Story*, *Toy Story 2*, or *Toy Story 3*.

Looking back on that close call, Ed Catmull said, "Two more inches—no Pixar."[1] But it's not just Pixar's animated movies that would have gone missing. Ed noted, with no small measure of satisfaction, how many Pixar employees have met, married, and had what he calls Pixar kids. "All those Pixar couples have no inkling of the two inches that could have kept them from meeting or their children from being conceived."[2]

Life is a game of inches!

It's two-inch events that change our trajectory.

After a few too many drinks, Dee Duncan was standing on a street corner in Georgetown at two o'clock in the morning. A cab pulled up, Dee got in the backseat, and the driver said, "You were doing something you shouldn't have been doing, weren't you?" That'll sober you up in a hurry!

The cabby-prophet said, "I never drive in this area of town, but the Lord told me to turn down this street, that there was someone He needed to talk to."

As he drove Dee across town to his apartment, he told him that God had a plan and purpose for his life. He also told him he needed to find a church. The very next day Dee walked into National Community Church for the first time. He started attending regularly, got plugged into a small group, and even went on a mission trip to Zambia with one of my children. But my favorite part of the story is the day he sat two inches from a girl named Anna. A few years later Dee got up on stage after one of our services, got down on one knee, and asked Anna if he could have her hand in marriage.

Now rewind the tape.

What if that taxi driver hadn't obeyed that little prompting to turn down *that street* at *that moment*? I don't think Dee would have found National Community Church. And while I don't want to belittle the sovereignty of God one iota, I'm not sure Dee would have found Christ or Anna either.

What I am sure of is this: God is in the business of strategically positioning us in the right place at the right time. Of course, it often seems like the wrong place at the wrong time. But like a grand master who strategically positions his pawns, bishops, kings, and queens, God is setting you up.

Let me put my cards on the table. I don't believe in coincidence, not if you are living a Spirit-led life. I believe in Providence. I believe in a sovereign God who is ordering your footsteps, preparing good works in advance, and making all things work together for good. Of course, some things won't make sense until we cross the space-time continuum and enter eternity. In the meantime don't worry about meeting the right person. Focus on becoming the right person. If you keep doing the right things day in and day out, God will hold up His end of the bargain!

Hardly a week goes by that I don't hear crazy stories about God's sovereignty. And some of them start out as mistakes, like Dee having a few too many drinks. I recently heard about a woman who ordered a single copy of *The Circle Maker,* but we accidently shipped her an entire case. I don't recall this, but evidently I told her to keep the case. She gave those books to people when she felt a prompting, and eight of them put their faith in Christ.

You can call it human error.

I call it supernatural synchronicity.

It may seem insignificant, but it's a providential preposition: Eleazar was *with* David when they taunted the Philistines. In other words, he was in the right place, at the right time, with the right person. And it was no coincidence. It was a two-inch event that changed the trajectory of his life.

I love the scene in *Back to the Future Part II* when Doc Brown says to Marty McFly, "Obviously the time continuum has been disrupted, creating a new temporal event sequence resulting in this alternate reality."[3]

It's not science fiction; it's fact.

It's not a script; it's Scripture.

It's not an accident; it's a divine appointment.

Can I make a simple observation? Notice who's next to you! What you think is a seat assignment might be a divine assignment. The person two inches away may change your destiny, or you might change theirs!

Just a Little Farther

As Taylor Wilkerson crossed the George Washington Bridge, he felt prompted to pray for the New York City neighborhood God had called him to. Harlem was the epicenter of a cultural renaissance in the 1920s, but the Great Depression, coupled with deindustrialization, left crime and poverty in its wake.

As Taylor circled Harlem in his car, the Lord kept telling him, *Just a little farther.* Ninety minutes later Taylor prayed one final prayer as he headed home: *Even now, Lord, give me an opportunity to reach someone.*

After parking his car Taylor hadn't taken five steps when he made eye contact with Michael. Taylor asked him a rather bold question: "Do you like your life?" Looking down at the ground, Michael said, "No. I hate my life. I messed it all up."

When Taylor asked Michael if he knew Jesus, Michael proudly revealed the chain around his neck. "Yeah. I keep Him around my neck." Taylor gently explained that wearing Jesus around your neck isn't enough, that you have to invite Him into your heart. Then Taylor asked Michael if he'd ever been to church.

"A few years ago I was in downtown Manhattan," Michael said, "when an old white dude stopped me and invited me to church. He was dressed all nice in a suit. Later that day I went there, and it turns out he was the pastor! Have you heard of Times Square Church?"

Taylor laughed to himself but kept a poker face. He asked Michael if he remembered the pastor's name. Michael said, "I gotta think about that. It was . . . Wilkerson. Yeah, David Wilkerson." Then Taylor tipped his hand. "Do you want to know my name? My name is Taylor David Wilkerson. Michael, the last person to tell you about Jesus was my great-uncle David Wilkerson. And now Jesus sent me to remind you that it's not too late to start over."

When God tells you to go "just a little farther," a divine appointment might be two inches or two seconds away. If you ignore the prompting, you miss the miracle. If you obey the prompting, you get to go down the rabbit hole. Nothing sets us up for a miracle like going the extra mile—"just a little farther." That's when God shows up and shows off. One small step of faith can turn into a giant leap. One chase can change the trajectory of your life or someone else's eternity.

Taylor shared that story with me over a cup of coffee. He and his wife, Kristen, also shared their heart for Harlem. As they did, I had flashbacks to our first year of church planting in Washington, DC. Planting a church ranks as the scariest thing I've ever done, but fear, properly channeled, is scary awesome!

My wife's family, the Schmidgalls, have been friends with Taylor's family, the Wilkersons, for many decades. Taylor's dad, Rich Wilkerson, was like a brother to my father-in-law, Bob Schmidgall. So Taylor and Kristen feel like cousins. They are as nice as nice can be, but make no mistake about it, they are lion chasers! I see a fierce faith within them that is epitomized by one prophetic prayer. Almost like Elisha asking for Elijah's mantle, Taylor prayed, *Lord, if there be any unanswered prayer or unfulfilled dream in David Wilkerson's life, answer it through me!*

Taylor and Kristen's dream, Trinity Harlem, is really a dream within a dream. It traces back to a near-death experience—a two-inch encounter when David Wilkerson stared death in the face without flinching.

Hold that thought.

Fifty-Year-Old Dreams

A year after the attack on the Twin Towers, I made a trip to New York City with my mentor, Dick Foth, and our friend John Ashcroft. The attorney general had been invited to be a guest on the *Late Show with David Letterman,* and he invited us to be his guests. It was a fun experience, but meeting David Letterman wasn't the most memorable part of the trip. It was an impromptu meeting with David Wilkerson, the founding pastor of Times Square Church. Like earthquake aftershocks, that ten-minute conversation still reverberates in my spirit.

David Wilkerson's raw transparency was disarming as he talked about the way Matthew 25 was messing with his mind. He wondered aloud if he would hear God say, "Well done, good and faithful servant!" He questioned whether he'd been "faithful with a few things" or "loved the least of these." I could hardly believe what I was hearing.

David Wilkerson felt called to the gangs of New York in the 1950s. When they threatened to kill him, he refused to back down. The most famous confrontation is recorded in *The Cross and the Switchblade,* the *New York Times* bestseller that has sold more than fifteen million copies.

When Nicky Cruz, the warlord of the Mau Mau street gang, got up in David's face and threatened to kill him, David said, "You can cut me into a thousand pieces and lay them out in the street, and every piece will still love you."

David Wilkerson was a lion chaser, to say the least! Yet he wondered aloud whether he had loved the least of these, in the spirit of Matthew 25.

As he shared his doubts about living up to the gospel gold standard, I couldn't help but think, *If David Wilkerson doesn't hear, "Well done, good and faithful servant," I'm in big trouble!*

I had a flashback to that ten-minute meeting with David when Taylor told me that his driving passion is Matthew 25—feeding the hungry, clothing the naked, caring for the sick. He's fulfilling his great-uncle's fifty-year-old dream. And there's one more piece to the dream puzzle. While reading *The Cross and the Switchblade*, Taylor discovered that David had dreamed of planting a church in Harlem, which he never did. Trinity Harlem isn't just Taylor's dream. It's a fulfillment of a dream that his great-uncle had five decades before.

It's a dream within a dream.

Premove

One of the most humbling yet rewarding moments in a parent's life is when "the student becomes the teacher." I had one of those moments with my son Parker a few years back. He had beaten me in chess quite a few times but never in three moves! He called it the Queen's Gambit; I called it *lucky*. But truth be told, Parker had been studying opening moves, forcing moves, quiet moves, and countermoves.

Did you know the total number of possible permutations in just the first ten moves of a chess game is 169,518,829,100,544,000,000,000,000,000? I'd spell it out, but neither of us has that kind of time![4]

That's a lot of contingencies and possibilities. And the game of life is far more complicated than a game of chess. But that shouldn't make you nervous, not if the Grand Master is the One ordering your footsteps. After all, it's in Him that we "live and *move* and have our being."[5]

The key to success is making the right moves, and it's helpful to think in chess terms. Our move to Washington, DC, was a *quiet move*, but that one move set the table for the next twenty years. Our first service was an *opening move*, but it wasn't any more spectacular than moving a pawn one space. When the DC public school where we met closed down because of fire-code violations, our move to the movie theaters at Union Station was a *countermove*. And launching our second campus was a *forcing move* that led to a third, a fourth, and eventually an eighth campus.

As I survey all the possible permutations, it's a little overwhelming. What if we had done *this* instead of *that*? What if we had gone *here* instead of *there*? And what if we had done it *sooner* instead of *later*? But I see a common thread in our storyline: one move set up the next move, which set up the move after that. In chess it's called a *premove*—it's the move before the move before the move.

We didn't move to Washington, DC, to plant a church, but God had ulterior motives. We thought we were moving to DC to lead an inner-city ministry, and we were. But God always has reasons beyond reason. The move to DC was a premove. God was setting me up to pastor National Community Church.

Thinking back on all the possible permutations makes me a little dizzy, but I find my equilibrium in God's sovereignty. Everything in our past is a premove, and God will use it for His glory somehow, someway.

Your birth date and birthplace were no accident. It was the opening move in a life that is destined to serve God's eternal plans and purposes. God determined exactly when and where you would be born.[6] And He's ordained every zip code thereafter.

I was in the eighth grade when our family started attending Calvary Church, and I didn't know the pastor had a daughter. And at that point I didn't care. That isn't why we went there, but the Matchmaker was setting me up. It was a premove. And when I met Lora, I pulled out my moves! I made opening moves, quiet moves, and counter moves until I checkmated my queen!

Closed Doors

For thirteen years National Community Church met in the movie theaters at Union Station, the transportation hub of Washington, DC that a hundred thousand people passed through every day. That not only put us in the middle of the marketplace, but it also put us on the map. Not many churches have their own Metro stop, train station, and taxi stand that drop people off at their front door!

That golden opportunity started with a phone call informing me that the DC public school where we met was closing its doors because of fire-code violations. My immediate reaction was fear, because it put us on the verge of becoming a homeless church. But I soon discovered that some of God's best premoves are closed doors.

I would not have walked into the movie theaters at Union Station if God hadn't closed that door. And it's no coincidence that I walked in the day after that theater chain rolled out a nationwide VIP program to recruit use of their theaters during nonmovie hours. It was as if God rolled out the red carpet, but the reality is, He had made premoves a century before.

After signing the lease with the movie theaters at Union Station, I picked up *Union Station: A History of Washington's Grand Terminal.* On February 28, 1903, Teddy Roosevelt signed "a bill of Congress to create a Union Station *and for other* purposes." That little phrase jumped off the page and into my spirit, infusing me with a sense of destiny.

Nearly a hundred years after that bill was passed, Union Station started serving *God's purposes* through the ministry of National Community Church. Roosevelt thought he was building a train station, but he was also building a church—and Congress funded our capital campaign!

Looking back, I laugh at the fact that I was so scared when the school we were meeting at closed. I even have the journal entry where I wrote that we had been "backed into a corner." It felt as if we had fallen into a pit with a lion on a snowy day. I couldn't see a way out, a way forward. And the same thing happened thirteen years later when I got a phone call informing me that the movie theaters at Union Station were shutting down. At first I was scared, just as I had been when the school shut down. How do you relocate a congregation that has grown into the thousands? And we had to do it in one week's time!

One of the most circled promises in my Bible is Revelation 3:7: "What he opens no one can shut, and what he shuts no one can open." I love the first half of that promise—open doors. The second half? Not so much! But some of the greatest miracles in my life have been on the other side of a closed door. It was the closed door at Union Station that led to our future campus—the $29.3 million Castle on Capitol Hill. So praise God for both!

Someday you may thank God for the closed doors even more than the open doors! It's one of His best premoves.

One Article

Albert Schweitzer was a twentieth-century renaissance man—doctor, philosopher, and organist extraordinaire. He signed with Columbia Records and produced twenty-five recordings of Johann Sebastian Bach. But it was his work as a medical missionary that earned him the Nobel Peace Prize in 1952. That entrepreneurial enterprise began in the spring of 1913 when Albert and his wife, Helene, traveled fourteen days by raft up the Ogooué River, through the Central African rainforest, to reach a mission outpost in Gabon. There they established a hospital and cared for tens of thousands of patients over four decades and through two world wars. A hundred years later Albert Schweitzer Hospital is one of the leading research hospitals on the continent of Africa and is working to end the scourge of malaria.[7]

Now here's the rest of the story.

One autumn day in 1904 Albert sat down at his writing desk at St. Thomas Seminary and found a magazine from the Paris Evangelical Missionary Society. It was put there by Miss Scherdlin, a childhood friend of Albert's. She knew that he loved those missionary letters. In fact, when he was a child, his father used to read them to him. Before turning to his studies, Albert turned the pages of that magazine until he came to an article titled "The Needs of the Congo Mission." That article changed the trajectory of his life. The author, Alfred Boegner, expressed hope that his appeal for missionaries would fall into the hands of those "on whom the Master's eyes already rested."

Albert Schweitzer had locked eyes with his lion. "I finished my article," Schweitzer said, "and quietly began my work. My search was over."[8]

It was a quiet move, a premove.

I don't belong in the same sentence as Schweitzer, but my dream journey parallels his in one significant way. Like Schweitzer, I discovered my destiny in a magazine. On the heels of our failed church plant during my seminary days, I was flipping through a mission magazine when I came across an advertisement for a parachurch ministry in Washington, DC. Why I stopped flipping the pages is still a mystery to me, but there was something magnetic about that particular page. That article led to a phone call, which led to a visit, which led to an opening move to Washington, DC.

Destiny doesn't make appointments. It usually shows up at the door unannounced. And it often knocks quietly, so you have to listen carefully. It shows up in a magazine, in a meeting, in a lecture. It shows up on vacation or on a mission trip.

In a sense, you don't discover your destiny. Your destiny discovers you. It shows up in a field of lentils, in taunting Philistines, in a pit with a lion on a snowy day.

I don't know what Benaiah had on his to-do list that day, but I'm sure he had places to go and things to do. But Benaiah recognized his destiny when it roared. Instead of taking flight, he decided to fight for his destiny.

The Learning Curve

The genesis moment of Albert Schweitzer's dream was the autumn day in 1904 when he picked up a magazine from the Paris Evangelical Missionary Society. But let me reverse-engineer his dream journey a little further. It was a summer morning in 1896 when Albert made a resolution.

"While outside the birds sang . . . I came to the conclusion that until I was thirty I could consider myself justified in devoting myself to scholarship and the arts," Schweitzer said, "but after that I would devote myself directly to serving humanity."[9]

I like Schweitzer's approach to the third decade of life: learn as much as you can about as much as you can. I've shared that philosophy with our congregation, which is 50 percent single twenty-somethings. Don't put too much pressure on yourself to climb the corporate ladder. For most people their first job is not their dream job, and neither is their second or third or fourth. But that's part of the process of discovering our destiny. It's those odd jobs and unenjoyable jobs that help us identify our dream job once we find it.

Instead of climbing the corporate ladder, focus on the learning curve.

That's what Nicole Poindexter did when she was between jobs. Instead of fixating on the fact that she was jobless, she decided to make the most of it. One of her New Year's resolutions was reading the Bible cover to cover, but Nicole had so much time on her hands and so much hunger in her heart that she finished by the end of January!

Nicole connected with the promises of God in a way she never had before. And it seemed like every move she made was ordained by God. In Nicole's words, "Nothing that happened in that month was coincidence."

During her self-made sabbatical, Nicole started researching solar-powered electricity as a potential business on the continent of Africa. One month later she was on a plane to Ghana.

> On the last day of my trip, it was Ghanaian Independence Day, and I was asked to stop in at a prayer service for the country. As I watched the room full of people praying, I realized that it was easy to make this dream about me and my success, but I knew that God had brought me to Ghana to be a blessing to them.

The first verses Nicole memorized after putting her faith in Christ was the promise given to Abraham in Genesis 12:1–2: "Go from your country, your people and your father's household to the land I will show you. . . . I will bless you . . . and you will be a blessing."

That verse is Nicole's script, and she is living it out literally—leaving her country and going to the country that God has shown her. In 2015, 125 Africans in the village of Affulkrom got electricity for the first time in their lives, thanks to Nicole's dream. Four months and four villages later, the total was up to 750 people. As Nicole likes to say, "The score is now

Light 750, Darkness 0." That solar-powered electricity is a lifeline, enabling everything from communication to health care.

If you don't have a dream, keep learning while you're waiting.

Get into God's Word, and God's dream will get into you.

Dream Year

A few years into our church plant, I met a fellow church planter in the DC area named Ben Arment. We struck up a friendship, which is easy for church planters because it can be a lonely journey.

At the time, I was a conference junkie. I was always looking for ideas that our staff could beg, borrow, or steal, and we got lots of them at the Catalyst Conference in Atlanta, Georgia. The first year we attended, only two of us went, but that conference became an annual pilgrimage for our staff. It was part of our learning curve. The last time we made the trip, more than fifty staff members attended. In all those years, only once did we take someone who was *not* a staff member. That person was Ben Arment, and I felt prompted to pay his way.

"That one trip changed my life," Ben said. "All my dreams and desires found resonance at that event." What I didn't know at the time is that Ben had taken a small step of faith by incorporating an organization that would produce conferences much like Catalyst.

The Catalyst Conference is a big event—thirteen-thousand people pack the Gwinnett Center every year. But for Ben it was a two-inch event. It took courage for Ben to quit pastoring. But he realized that he was "wired to launch things, not to pastor people."

The dream of creating conferences didn't happen overnight. In fact, Ben renewed the annual fee on his dream ten times before he finally gave birth to his brainchild, the STORY conference. Sometimes that's how long it takes for our expertise and our experiences to catch up with our dreams!

I miss more opportunities than I seize, trust me, but I knew that Ben needed to go to that conference with us. I thought it would help him fulfill his calling as a pastor, but God had a surprise up His sovereign sleeve. Catalyst became the catalyst for Ben to quit pastoring and start pursuing other God-given, God-ordained dreams.

Over the past decade Ben has helped countless people pursue their dreams through the STORY conference and his coaching network, Dream Year.[10] And in keeping with the way he's wired, Ben has since sold those ventures to chase even bigger lions!

"Once a lion chaser," Ben says, "always a lion chaser!"

THE DECISIVE MOMENT

But Eleazar stood his ground.

2 Samuel 23:10

ON SEPTEMBER 2, 2015, the dead body of a three-year-old Syrian boy named Aylan Kurdi washed ashore near the port city of Bodrum, Turkey. He had been fleeing from the Islamic State with his refugee family, seeking sanctuary in Europe. A Turkish journalist, Nilüfer Demir, snapped photos of Aylan's lifeless body lying in the wet sand and of a refugee worker carrying his limp little body.

Those images offended the public consciousness and drew attention to the greatest refugee crisis since World War II. Nations took notice, prayer vigils were held, and donations to refugee-related charities surged. "It was one of those moments," noted the BBC, "when the whole world seems to care."[1]

We have a choice in moments like this: go back to business as usual or be about the Father's business. Which is it? Because it's either one or the other.

Syria has a population of twenty-three million people, and nearly half of them are displaced and in desperate need of humanitarian help. Half of that half are innocent children, like Aylan.

An old adage says, "A picture is worth a thousand words." But I think it's worth more than that. The brain processes print on a page at one hundred bits per second, while it processes pictures at one billion bits per second. So technically, a picture is really worth ten million words![2]

"Photojournalists sometimes capture images so powerful," said Nick

Logan of *Global News,* "the public and policymakers can't ignore what the
pictures show."[3] One picture has the power to prick the conscience. It can
start a riot or start a revolution.

Famed photographer Henri Cartier-Bresson called it "the decisive moment." He not only coined the phrase, but he also wrote a best-selling book
by that title. "To me," he said, "photography is the simultaneous recogni-
tion, in a fraction of a second, of the significance of an event." If you are a
split second early or a split second late, you miss the moment. And it's not to
be left to luck. To Cartier-Breeson, it was a learned skill requiring an eye for
the occasion. "You must know with intuition when to click the camera," he
said. "Once you miss it, it is gone forever." But if you capture it? "A photograph [can] fix eternity in an instant."[4]

If the Bible were a picture book, 2 Samuel 23 would have more than its
fair share of decisive moments. I can picture Josheb-Basshebeth raising his
spear with eight hundred enemy soldiers in the blurred background. I can
picture the look on Benaiah's face as he locks eyes with the lion. But let me
zoom in on Eleazar's hand, the hand that froze to his sword when he took
his stand against the Philistines.

Eyes squint in the midday sun.

Jaw muscles clench tight.

Veins in his sword arm pulsate.

It's Clint Eastwood in *Sudden Impact*: "Go ahead, make my day!"

It's John Wayne in *True Grit*: "Young fella, if you're looking for trouble,
I'll accommodate you."

It's Russell Crowe in *Gladiator*: "My name is Maximus Decimus
Meridius, commander of the Armies of the North, General of the Felix
Legions and loyal servant to the true emperor, Marcus Aurelius. Father to a
murdered son, husband to a murdered wife. And I will have my vengeance,
in this life or the next."

I don't want to put words in Eleazar's mouth, and his actions speak
louder than words anyway. But if I'm the scriptwriter, this is the moment for
Eleazar's epic one-liner. And I'm guessing he said something like this: "I
may die on this battlefield today, but I won't die with a sword in my back!"

The word *retreat* wasn't in Eleazar's vocabulary. Neither was *defeat*. It wasn't fight or flight. It was fight for your life, fight to the death!

I recently spoke at a pastor's conference in Harrogate, England.[5] Speaking right after Archbishop of Canterbury Justin Welby was awfully humbling. But not as humbling as speaking before Brother Edward, who pastors a church in Damascus, the capital of Syria. A few weeks before the conference, 157 people were killed in a bombing not far from where he pastors. His life is in danger every day. His congregants walk down sniper alleys just to worship together.

There goes any excuse we have!

The moderator of the conference asked Brother Edward why he doesn't leave Syria. "When one country pulls its ambassadors out of another country, you know it's bad," said Brother Edward. "God is not calling His ambassadors out of Syria."

Like Eleazar before him, Brother Edward holds his ground.

A Hundred Generations

Every life is defined by decisive moments, and those moments of decision often dictate the course of decades. That shouldn't make you nervous, not if God is ordering your footsteps. It should fill you with a sense of destiny!

In his book *Decisive Moments in History,* author Stefan Zweig described "a single moment that determines and decides everything: a single *Yes,* a single *No,* a *too early* or a *too late* makes that hour irrevocable for a hundred generations and determines the life of an individual, a people, and even the destiny of all mankind."[6]

That may sound like an overstatement at first, but I actually think it's an understatement. Yes, decisive moments are few and far between. But the ripple effects of those moments transcend time and space. Our actions and inactions have eternal ramifications. And for the record, inaction *is* an action.

When we fail to take action, we forfeit the future. And just as inaction is an action, indecision is a decision. As Edmund Burke famously said, "The only thing necessary for the triumph of evil is for good men to do nothing."[7] It's true of the refugee crisis and every other crisis our world faces. It's our job as lion chasers to step up, to step in. Do we need immigration laws and asylum policies? Absolutely. But we also need to fulfill our diplomatic duty as ambassadors of heaven.

NCC recently sent a team to work with our friends at the A21 Campaign who are providing relief, with lots of love, in refugee camps outside Thessaloniki, Greece. My wife, Lora, spent several days in one of those camps, and the pictures she took of those precious children, children like Aylan, were heartbreaking. With each picture I prayed, *God, help us help them!*

Sometimes it feels as if hope has been lost, but don't forget that history is broken in half by the birth of Christ. Quit living as though it's BC— before Christ. It's AD—*anno domini,* the year of the Lord. If you need to, reread the book of Revelation to remind yourself that love wins and hate loses; faith wins and fear loses!

We fight darkness with light, fear with faith, and hate with hope. And when we do, the gates of hell cannot prevail against us. In the words of Julia Ward Howe and her "Battle Hymn of the Republic," "Glory! Glory! Hallelujah! His truth is marching on!"[8]

His truth is unstoppable!

His grace is unconquerable!

But we must step up, step in.

Silver Spoon

Elizabeth Fry was born with a silver spoon in her mouth, yet she refused to turn a blind eye to the Dickensian poverty of nineteenth-century London. A contemporary of William Wilberforce, who led the campaign to abolish slavery in Great Britain, Elizabeth Fry had two great objectives. The first was prison reform, and the second was homelessness. And both were five-hundred-pound lions!

One day a family friend, Stephen Grellet, invited Elizabeth to visit

Newgate Prison. The conditions she encountered in the women's ward hor-rified her. Elizabeth had eleven children of her own to care for, but that didn't keep her from caring for those prisoners. She returned the next day with food and clothes. Then she started a prison school for the children of those female prisoners. And eventually she founded the British Ladies' So-ciety for Promoting the Reformation of Female Prisoners, the first nation-wide women's organization in England. Fry's strategy for raising awareness was inviting prominent members of society to spend a night in prison—in a pit—so they could experience the conditions for themselves.[9]

In the winter of 1819, Elizabeth stumbled upon the body of a young boy who had frozen to death.[10] Much like the photograph of Aylan Kurdi, it was an image she would never forget. Elizabeth established a nightly shel-ter to care for the homeless of London, a model that was replicated all across Great Britain.

A great dream doesn't just make a difference. It inspires dreams to the third and fourth generation. And that may be Elizabeth's greatest legacy. In 1840 at the age of sixty, Elizabeth started a training school for nurses. It was that program that inspired Florence Nightingale, the mother of modern nursing, to step up and step in during the Crimean War. Like doctors who swear to uphold the Hippocratic Oath, nurses vow the Nightingale Pledge.[11] They may not know the full backstory, since the pledge was instituted in 1893, but their vow is a dream within a dream.

Since 2001 Elizabeth Fry has been pictured on the Bank of England's five-pound note. That's a high honor. It's a testimony to a woman who sim-ply refused to remain silent, who refused to do nothing.

Don't let what you cannot do keep you from doing what you can.

Don't give up before you give it a try.

Hold your ground or hold your peace? Which is it?

Contextual Intelligence

In the book *In Their Time,* Anthony Mayo and Nitin Nohria profile some of the greatest business leaders of the twentieth century. Those leaders lived in different eras, worked in different industries, and faced different challenges, but the authors found one common denominator among them—*contextual intelligence.* It's the differentiating factor between success and failure in for-profit and nonprofit dreams. Great leaders possess acute sensitivity to the social, political, technological, and demographic contexts that define their eras.

It was true of Steve Jobs, who had a vision for an all-in-one computer in every home. It was true of Elizabeth Fry, who fought for social reform in nineteenth-century England. And it was true of David's mighty men, who led a political revolt in the tenth century BC.

Let me put contextual intelligence into biblical context:

From the tribe of Issachar, there were 200 leaders of the tribe with their relatives. All these men understood the signs of the times and knew the best course for Israel to take.[12]

For the record, the other tribes are referred to as *warriors* or *soldiers.* Only those from the tribe of Issachar are called *leaders.*[13] Why? Because of their contextual intelligence. They didn't just have a pulse on the social, political, and spiritual temper of the times. They were innovators and entrepreneurs who knew how to turn their ideas into strategies.

Contextual intelligence is the ability to spot opportunity where others don't. That's what sets leaders apart; that's what sets them up for success. Call it a sixth sense. Call it gut instinct. Lion chasers see and seize the decisive moment.

In 1893 a $10,000 Congressional appropriation established Rural Free Delivery. Until then Americans living in rural areas rode their horses into town to pick up their mail at the general store. RFD provided mail service to rural residents for the first time. Two enterprising businessmen, Aaron Montgomery Ward and Richard Sears, saw a new distribution channel for their products. They produced so many catalogs that they became the second most widely read books in the country after the Bible.[14]

That's contextual intelligence.

Two thousand years ago Jesus said, "Go and make disciples of all nations."[15] He gave us a green light, but He didn't tell us *how* to go. For the better part of twenty centuries, it was on foot, on horseback, or by ship. Now we go by plane, train, and automobile. We can even "go" at the speed of light, circumnavigating the globe six times per second with a digital gospel.

The game has changed, but the rules haven't. *There are ways of doing church that no one has thought of yet.* We shouldn't just be trend spotters. With the Holy Spirit's help, we should be trendsetters. If you want to reach people no one is reaching, you might have to do something no one else is doing. To be clear, the gospel doesn't require gimmicks. In the same breath, irrelevance is irreverence. Innovation is a form of incarnation. And anything less is laziness!

What does that have to do with Eleazar?

What I see in Eleazar is a man who understood the times. He not only saw an opportunity, but he seized it. He didn't shrink in fear. He stepped up, stepped in. And most important, he knew what battlefield he was willing to die on.

As a dreamer, you have to choose your battles wisely. There are lots of kingdom causes that I care deeply about, but I can't devote my time, talent, and treasure to all of them. I can't be on the front lines of every fight. Sometimes I cheer others on from the sidelines with my giving, my praying. But like Eleazar, you need to identify the battlefield you're willing to die on. Then you need to fight the good fight until your hand freezes to the sword.

Kodak Moment

For nearly a hundred years, the Eastman Kodak company dominated the film industry. Not only did it control 85 percent of camera sales, but it was ranked one of the five most valuable brands in America.[16]

In 1996 Kodak had 140,000 employees and a valuation of $28 billion. A decade later they stopped turning a profit. And in 2012 Kodak filed for bankruptcy.[17]

The question is, what happened?

In 1975 a small team of talented technicians at Kodak built the first digital camera. It was the size of a toaster, weighed 8.5 pounds, and had a resolution of .01 megapixels.[18] It also took twenty-three seconds to snap the picture! Makes you appreciate your camera phone, doesn't it? Kodak was on the cutting edge of technology, but they didn't jump the curve. Instead of embracing the new technology, they decided to do it the way it had always been done. In other words, they missed the decisive moment while they were in the darkroom. Or you could even say they missed the *Kodak moment.*

In his brilliant book *The Anointing,* R. T. Kendall talks about the danger of becoming what he calls *yesterday's man.* People who had a tremendous anointing on their lives yesterday can live off the momentum of that anointing for a while. Some people even think the anointing is still on them, but it's the momentum of yesterday's anointing.[19]

I read a one-liner on page 133 of his book that packed a punch. It influenced me the way page 23 in *Fresh Wind, Fresh Fire* influenced Steven Furtick. "Sometimes the greatest opposition to what God wants to do next," said R. T. Kendall, "comes from those who were on the cutting edge of what God did last."[20]

I need God's anointing *today* more than I did *yesterday.* And I'll need it even more *tomorrow* than I do *today!* Without it, I'm below average, and I'll eventually become yesterday's man. With it, the law of averages is out the window! We don't just let the future happen; we make it happen with God's help.

What got you here might not get you where you need to go next. At critical junctures you have to jump the curve. You have to reinvent yourself, reimagine your life. That's what dreamers do.

This past year I took my first true sabbatical in twenty years, a three-month hiatus to rest and read and recreate. Just prior to my last sermon before sabbatical, our staff surprised me with a thank-you video that made my eyes sweat. After watching it with me, my youngest son, Josiah, said, "Dad, you better be inspirational."

No pressure!

Truth be told, I embrace the pressure that puts on me. In fact, I think it's healthy and holy. Excellence honors God, so we need to get better and better at whatever we're called to do. And it happens little by little, day by day. That positive stress, eustress, forces me to seek a fresh anointing each and every day. Without it, I'm coasting. With it, I'm gaining momentum.

Inertia

One final thought from Henri Cartier-Bresson: "There is nothing in this world that does not have a decisive moment."[21] That's true of companies, like Kodak. And it's true of people, like Eleazar, like you.

Let me share one more decisive moment, because it might help you identify yours.

A 1999 poll by the British journal *Physics World* ranked Richard Feynman as one of the ten greatest physicists of all time.[22] Winner of the 1965 Nobel Prize for physics, Feynman popularized his passion for quantum physics via lectures, books, and his famous Feynman diagrams.

Before he was even born, his father prophetically stated, "If it's a boy, he's going to be a scientist." When Richard was a baby, his father would set up tiles like dominoes, and baby Richard would push them over. It was his first lesson in physics. When Richard was a small boy, his father would set him on his lap and read to him from the *Encyclopaedia Britannica*.

The greatest gift Richard Feynman's father bequeathed to him was the ability to notice things. One day Richard was pulling a little wagon when he became intrigued with the way a ball in the wagon would roll. When he pulled the wagon, the ball rolled to the back. When he stopped, the ball rolled to the front. When he asked why, his father said, "That, nobody knows."

It was Richard's dad daring him to figure out why.

He then explained, "Things which are moving tend to keep on moving, and things which are standing still tend to stand still, unless you push them hard. This tendency is called inertia."

It was a decisive moment for Richard Feynman.

Looking back on that boyhood memory, Feynman said, "It has motivated me for the rest of my life."[23] In a sense, Feynman's entire career was an attempt to answer that genesis question. And it's that kind of laser-like focus that is absolutely necessary when chasing a five-hundred-pound lion. One misstep can end a dream journey. That doesn't mean you operate in a spirit of fear. It does mean you operate in a spirit of focus!

Every step needs to be carefully measured at critical junctures. Like a good carpenter, you need to *measure twice and cut once*. If you measure only once, you'll probably have to cut twice! Of course, if you're afraid of making a mistake, you'll probably miss the opportunity. So it's a balancing act.

There are opportunities all around you all the time—opportunities to show kindness, opportunities to show courage. And just like the photographer who is ready to click and capture the moment, you have to be ready to seize the opportunity.

Gut Instincts

One of the most impressive feats in professional sports is hitting a baseball that is 2.86 inches in diameter and traveling 60.5 feet in .43 seconds.[24] It takes one-fifth of a second for the retina to receive incoming messages, and by then the ball is halfway to home plate![25] The margin of error between hitting and missing the ball is only five milliseconds.

What's true of baseball players is also true of sword fighters. Peripheral vision and reaction time are critical! But instead of three strikes and you're out, it is one miss and you're dead.

Even the best baseball hitters don't really see the pitch. They have to swing long before they know when or where the ball will be. They aren't seeing it as much as they are seeing into the future. They are guessing, based on visual clues, when and where the pitch will cross the plate.

It reminds me of the famous quip by hockey great Wayne Gretzky. His secret to success? "I skate to where the puck is going to be, not where it has been."[26] And what's true in hockey is also true in chess.

In a 1940s study of chess players, Dutch psychologist Adriaan de Groot tried to discern what differentiated chess masters from grand masters. One difference he discovered was their ability to anticipate moves. Grand masters had a better understanding of the game situation in *five seconds* than club players had in fifteen minutes.[27]

What does that have to do with Eleazar?

And what does that have to do with you?

Over time we cultivate a sixth sense that enables us to operate out of instinct. Whether you play professional football or the stock market, experience leads to instincts. And those gut instincts can make or break you. At times you have to ignore your instincts. But more often than not, you need to obey your gut instincts. And that takes good old-fashioned guts.

If Eleazar had calculated the odds, doing a thorough cost-benefit analysis, he probably would have run away with the rest of the retreaters. But Eleazar had a few battles under his belt. He not only trusted his training. He trusted his gut instincts, and they were gutsy!

I could have told you a dozen different stories about decisive moments, but I chose Richard Feynman's story because it revolves around the idea of *inertia*. Inertia is the resistance of a physical object to a change in its state of motion. And that's especially true of physical objects called human beings.

When it comes to chasing lions, inertia is enemy number one. Our natural tendency is to think the way we've always thought and do things the way we've always done them. It's hard to break old habits and hard to build new habits. But if you want God to do something new, you can't keep doing the same old thing.

What do you need to stop doing today?

What do you need to start doing today?

Whether it's a stop-doing list or a start-doing list, a dream without a to-do list is called a wish list. Don't get overwhelmed by the size of the lion. Focus on the first step.

If you don't do it, you'll become *yesterday's man*.

But if you do it, you'll become *tomorrow's man, tomorrow's woman*.

FROZEN

Till his hand grew tired and froze to the sword

2 Samuel 23:10

ON THE AFTERNOON OF APRIL 18, 1946, Jackie Robinson made his debut as the first black player in the modern era of the major leagues. He hit a three-run homer over the left-field fence in the third inning of his first game. As he crossed home plate, the batter up, George Shuba, extended his hand in a congratulatory gesture. An Associated Press photographer captured that decisive moment. It was one small handshake, one giant leap for racial equity in professional sports.[1]

George "Shotgun" Shuba went on to play seven seasons for the Brooklyn Dodgers and was on the 1955 World Series championship team.

In his celebrated baseball book, *The Boys of Summer,* Roger Kahn said Shuba's swing was "as natural as a smile."[2] Shuba laughed at Kahn's description. During an interview with Kahn, Shuba walked over to a filing cabinet and pulled out a chart marked with lots of Xs. During the off-season, Shuba would swing a weighted bat six hundred times a day. And that was after working his off-season job all day! Every night he'd take sixty swings and then mark an X on his chart. After ten Xs, he'd give himself permission to go to bed. Shuba practiced that daily ritual for fifteen years!

"You call that natural?" Shuba asked Kahn. "I swung a 44-ounce bat 600 times a night, 4,200 times a week, 47,200 swings every winter."[3]

In my humble opinion, no one is a natural. Sure, some people are more naturally gifted than others. But unless that giftedness is coupled with a complementary work ethic, it'll only result in wasted potential.

You can't just pray as if it depends solely on God; you also have to work as if it depends on you. It's your work ethic plus your prayer ethic that will inch you closer to your dream. And it happens one practice, one day at a time.

That mind-set is exemplified by actor Will Smith's not-so-secret secret to success:

> I'm not afraid to die on a treadmill. I will not be outworked. You may be more talented than me. You might be smarter than me. And you may be better looking than me. But if we get on a treadmill together you are going to get off first or I'm going to die.[4]

That's how the *Fresh Prince of Bel-Air* star became one of Hollywood's most bankable actors. It wasn't on talent alone. It was on the treadmill.

Are you willing to die on the treadmill? That's the difference between chasing and catching the five-hundred-pound lion. You can't outrun it, but you can outwork it. You can't outsmart it, but you can outlast it.

No matter what dream you are chasing, there are no shortcuts. You have to do your homework. For Shotgun Shuba it was swinging a bat. For Will Smith it was dress rehearsals. For Eleazar it was sparring matches.

I'm not sure how a person's hand freezes to a sword, but I love that depiction. It's the ancient equivalent of dying on a treadmill. No one could outlast Eleazar. And that set the stage for the next sentence of Scripture: "The LORD brought about a great victory that day."[5]

That day must have been one of the greatest days of Eleazar's life! But I would submit that the day he won the victory wasn't the day he won the victory. He won the victory the day before, and the day before the day before. Just as David defeated Goliath while fighting lions and bears as a shepherd, Eleazar defeated his foe long before they met on the battlefield.

This could be the greatest year of your life, your dream year, but you have to *win the day*. That's how you win the week, win the month, win the year. No one achieves his or her dream without daily disciplines.

One at a Time

In a *Sports Illustrated* profile of two-time NFL MVP Aaron Rodgers, Peter King revealed the secret behind Rodger's success as the most efficient passer in NFL history. One statement says it all: "I desperately want to be coached."[6] It could be argued that no one needs to be coached less than Aaron Rodgers, yet no one wants to be coached more! That's a recipe for success in any endeavor.

Games aren't won on game day.

Games are won in the weight room, the film room, the locker room.

I often remind young pastors that God doesn't just want to anoint them in the pulpit. He also wants to anoint them in the study. And if they cheat God in the study, they can't expect Him to compensate for it in the pulpit. That goes for any occupation. If you cheat in med school, law school, or business school, I don't want you operating on me, representing me in court, or joint-venturing with me.

Before writing my first book, I read three thousand books. It was my way of paying the price, paying my dues. I also converted my sermons into "evotionals"—written versions of my sermons that I e-mailed to subscribers for many years. But it was less for subscribers than it was for me. It was my way of cultivating a writing discipline.

I don't know what dream you're chasing, but you have to prove yourself one swing, one rehearsal, one practice, one book at a time. And unless you want to be a one-hit wonder, you have to do it day in and day out.

Pablo Casals is considered by many to be the greatest cellist ever to draw the bow. He played for Queen Victoria when he was twenty-two. He also played for President Kennedy when he was eighty-six. Casals lived to the age of ninety-six, and he was still practicing three hours a day. When asked why, he said, "I'm beginning to notice some improvement."[7]

You get into shape one workout at a time.

You get out of debt one payment at a time.

You get your graduate degree one class at a time.

You get the music scholarship one rehearsal at a time.

You get the job promotion one project at a time.

You get the game ball one practice at a time.

Whatever dream journey you're on, you have to take it one step at a time. And if you keep doing the right things day in and day out, one day God is going to show up and show off.

Breakthrough Year

There was nothing easy, nothing glamorous about my first five years of pastoring. Just as some people live paycheck to paycheck, our church was surviving offering to offering. Growth did not come easy. We didn't have a hundred people at the end of our first year or two hundred people at the end of our second year. And according to many church-growth experts, that meant we might never break through those growth barriers. Of course, I'm not sure any of those experts had ever planted a church.

It took a lot longer than we wanted it to, and it was a lot harder than we thought it would be, but we proved the experts wrong. And you can too. It took us five years to grow from a core group of nineteen people into a congregation of two hundred and fifty people. Then miraculously we doubled in size during year six. It was our breakthrough year.

Here's how it happened.

In the summer of 2001, a reporter from the *Washington Post* contacted me because she'd heard about the unique demographics of our church. We were 80 percent single twenty-somethings at the time, which is an anomaly in the church world. In most churches millennials are missing in action.

After the interview the reporter told me the story would most likely make the Religion section that coming weekend. I walked into Union Station that following Sunday morning and made a beeline for the newsstand. I flipped through the newspaper like a kid on Christmas morning ripping through wrapping paper. This was our big break, our big moment. I found the Religion section, but I didn't find us in it. I even checked twice. To call it a big disappointment would be an understatement. I refolded the paper to put it back on the newsstand, because if we weren't in it, I certainly wasn't going to buy it. After all, the Sunday paper cost $1.25! That's when I spotted the article on the front page of the *Washington Post,* Sunday edition.

I used to joke that it must have been a slow news day for us to land on the front page of the *Washington Post.* I've since retracted that statement. It wasn't a slow news day. It was God's favor, God's timing. It was God's way of putting us on the map. In the weeks that followed, hundreds of people visited NCC because of that article. And what I love most about it is that I couldn't take one ounce of credit for it.

Long Obedience

We live in a culture that celebrates fifteen minutes of fame, but God honors a lifetime of faithfulness. The longer I live, the more I believe in *long obedience in the same direction.* That phrase encapsulates my philosophy of ministry, my philosophy of life. If you keep doing the right things day in and day out, look out. Somehow, someway, someday, God is going to show up and show off.

That's precisely what God did on August 12, 2001. After five years of our being faithful in the shadows, God put a spotlight on NCC. The favor we found was prefaced by five years of obedience in relative obscurity.

Obedience earns compound interest. Over time it's called faithfulness. And there is a cumulative effect. Eventually the blessings of God will overtake you.[8] God's Word does not return void.[9] He is watching over His word to perform it.[10] And He who began a good work will carry it to completion.[11]

You don't start over every day; you build on the day before.

John Wooden, the legendary basketball coach who won ten NCAA championships with the UCLA Bruins, lived by a simple creed: "Make each day your masterpiece."[12]

The way you chase a dream is by making each day your masterpiece. In short, *win the day!*

Win the practice. Win the class. Win the meeting.

Will you have bad days? Absolutely! But you need to minimize the losing streaks while maximizing the winning streaks. You need to practice daily rituals that will inch you closer to your dream. Then you need to stack those successes together. The net result is *long obedience in the same direction.*

That phrase originated with Friedrich Nietzsche, the German philosopher who announced the death of God. He couldn't have been more wrong on that count, but he couldn't have been more right on this count:

> The essential thing "in heaven and earth" is that there should be a long obedience in the same direction; there thereby results, and has always resulted in the long run, something which has made life worth living.[13]

We overestimate what we can accomplish in a year or two, but we underestimate what God can accomplish in a decade or two. If you're discouraged, zoom out. You can't just dream big; you have to think long. In fact, you need some life goals that will take a lifetime to accomplish. Maybe even a few that can't be accomplished!

One of my life goals, Life Goal #21, is to write twenty-five books. At an average pace of one book per year, it will take twenty-five years to accomplish that one goal. That goal helps me stay focused on the big picture, but I also try to celebrate each book as if it's the first and last book I'll write.

Dinner out on the day a book releases is a meaningful tradition. Then I'm back up, back at it the next day. Why? Because I'm only halfway to my goal of twenty-five books. And I don't believe I've written my best book yet.

Life Symbols

One of my favorite lines of lyrics is in the second verse of the 1758 hymn by Robert Robinson, "Come, Thou Fount of Every Blessing." Every time I sing it, I instinctively raise a clenched fist in worship.

Here I raise my Ebenezer.

After the Israelites pulled off an upset victory over the Philistines, the prophet Samuel built an altar and named it Ebenezer. It means "hitherto hath the LORD helped us."[14] An altar reminds us that the God who did it before can do it again. It's not just a token of God's faithfulness. It's a statement of faith: the God who got us *here* will get us *there,* and the God who did *this* will do *that.*

I don't know if Benaiah kept the lion skin or the spear that he ripped out of the Egyptian's hand, but I wouldn't be surprised if he did. And if he did, he was following David's example. After David defeated Goliath, he undressed the giant and hung his armor in his tent.[15] It's not insignificant that Scripture notes the exact weight of Goliath's armor—125 pounds, 15 ounces.[16] The armor might have weighed as much as David did!

So why would David go to all the trouble of hanging it in his tent? Because that armor doubled as a life symbol. It was a daily reminder of a defining moment in David's life. Every time the sunlight reflected off those bronze scales and caught the corner of David's eye, it renewed David's confidence in the God who is bigger than any giant we face.

After building our coffeehouse on Capitol Hill, we decided to name it Ebenezers. We were afraid some people would associate it with Ebenezer Scrooge, but it was a risk worth taking. There were so many miracles in the process of purchasing, rezoning, and building our coffeehouse that we wanted to name it what it is. Ebenezers is *not* a coffeehouse. Ebenezers is an altar to the God who helped us get where we are. And we just happen to serve coffee at this altar!

So Far So God

When Ebenezers was being built, I was invited to speak at a community meeting on Capitol Hill. I was nervous because I knew we needed the community's backing to get our property rezoned. I was also concerned that people would think of us as a *Christian* coffeehouse rather than a legit coffeehouse.

After sharing our vision for Ebenezers, I fielded questions. Someone asked me what *Ebenezers* meant, and I said that it basically meant "so far so good." But that isn't what it meant. And I knew it. I substituted *good* for *God,* when God is the One who miraculously gave it to us.

The bottom line? I chickened out.

A few weeks earlier we had hosted an Easter Eggtravaganza for several thousand kids and parents in our community, and one of the guests complained because she said we were talking about Jesus too much. We explained that National Community Church totally underwrote the event, we had permits from the National Park Service, and it was Easter after all. Oh, and then there's the Bill of Rights, which includes freedom of speech and freedom of religion. Even the free candy, petting zoo, and egg hunt didn't pacify her antagonism. So be it. Well, this woman was at the community meeting, and it put me in a defensive mind-set. So instead of offending this woman by saying *so far so God,* I offended the Holy Spirit.

Afterward I felt convicted by the Holy Spirit and my wife. Their voices sound very similar! I'm grateful for a godly wife who speaks the truth in love. After apologizing to God, I vowed that I would never play chicken again.

On our coffee sleeves at Ebenezers, there is a Scripture reference that looks like a SKU code—ISAM712. There are also the initials SFSG. The initials stand for "So Far So God." We took *good* out of the equation and added *God.*

In every dream journey there are Ebenezer moments. You have to celebrate those milestones by building altars. Then you have to surround yourself with those life symbols so you don't forget what God wants you to remember. That's why I have an old liquor bottle in my office. We found it in the crackhouse that we turned into Ebenezers coffeehouse. I also have a framed copy of the front-page article from the *Washington Post.*

I don't believe our greatest shortcoming is not feeling bad enough about what we've done wrong. I think our greatest shortcoming is not feeling good enough about what God has done right. When we undercelebrate, we fall short of the glory of God!

For some, Leviticus is their least favorite book in the Bible because of all the rules and regulations, but take a closer look. One of the *commands* was a seven-day celebration.[17] Question: When was the last time you celebrated anything for seven days? God challenged the Israelites to celebrate longer, to celebrate better! That's like a command to eat cupcakes. And God didn't just mandate weeklong celebrations. He also commanded a yearlong honeymoon for newlyweds!

> If a man has recently married, he must not be sent to war or have
> any other duty laid on him. For one year he is to be free to stay at
> home and bring happiness to the wife he has married.[18]

Hubba hubba!
That's another book for another day!
We need to celebrate more.
We need to celebrate better.
Why? Because hitherto the Lord has helped us!

Let It Go

To end a chapter titled "Frozen" without a story about the Disney film by the same name feels like a sin of omission. If you have an elementary-age daughter, you can skip to the next chapter without any judgment on my part whatsoever. I don't want to cause unnecessary emotional trauma because you've heard "Let It Go" a thousand times too many. The irony is that the moral of the song "Let It Go" is *not to let go*. You have to white knuckle your dreams like Queen Elsa and her ice-making abilities.

Written by the husband-and-wife songwriting team of Kristen Anderson-Lopez and Robert Lopez, "Let It Go" won an Academy Award for Best Original Song in 2014.[19] The powerful ballad was an instant hit, selling more than ten million copies in 2014. But what's easily forgotten is the fact that seventeen songs they wrote didn't make the cut.[20] Most of us give up after two or three rejections. But to achieve the highest level of success in any field, you need a high pain threshold when it comes to failure.

In order to write one hit song like "Let It Go," you have to write lots of songs! You have to swing the bat like George Shuba until you hit the charts. You have to get on the songwriting treadmill like Will Smith and not get off until you have a hit single.

When the London Philharmonic Orchestra selected the fifty greatest pieces of classical music, the list included six pieces by Mozart, five by Beethoven, and three by Bach. To generate those masterpieces, Mozart composed more than six hundred pieces, Beethoven produced six hundred and fifty, and Bach wrote more than a thousand pieces of music.[21]

If it had been baseball, Bach would have been batting .003! Total failure, right? Wrong!

That might not seem like a great batting average, but it takes lots of swings to get a hit. And like the other success stories in *Chase the Lion,* it takes a strong work ethic. We glamorize success, but it always comes back to basics. You have to practice scales, practice skills, practice techniques over and over and over again. And it will take lots of sacrifices, which usually starts with setting your alarm clock extra early in the morning!

How have Robert and Kristen achieved so much success in songwriting?

I love their answer: "First of all, we have to have a baby-sitter."[22]

Success is not sexy. It's sweaty!

Success is not glamorous. It's gritty!

Like Eleazar, you have to vice-grip your sword and keep fighting for your dream.

When it comes to discerning the will of God, I subscribe to a twofold litmus test.[23] You have to be *released from* and *called to.* And in my experience, the calling is easier to discern than the releasing.

Remember Ben Arment's dream of producing conferences? The hardest part was letting go of the church he had planted. But Ben had the courage to do it because he knew that God had released him. I came to the same conclusion during our attempted church plant in Chicago. And if I hadn't buried that dream in Chicago, my dream would never have been resurrected in Washington, DC.

If God has released you, then continuing to do what you've been doing isn't faithfulness. It's disobedience. You need to let it go. And don't look back.

If God hasn't released you, don't let go! You have to hang in there. And when it feels as though you can't hold on any longer, remember Eleazar, whose hand literally froze to the sword. That should help you hang in there a little longer!

FIELD OF DREAMS

There was a field full of lentils.

2 Samuel 23:11

JOEL MALM WAS ICE-AXING his way up Mount Elbrus, the highest peak in Europe. A whiteout made it impossible to summit. It also covered the trail markers back down the mountain. Joel had never felt more alive, more alert.

At sixteen thousand feet he could have chalked it up to oxygen deprivation, but Joel knew it was a vision from God. The thrill of conquering a mountain was more than an emotional high. It deepened his dependence upon God in a way that nothing else could. And that was the gift he wanted to give to other leaders like him. That's why Joel started Summit Leaders.[1]

Why go to a conference and passively listen to a leader when you can hike the Inca Trail or raft the Colorado River with him? I've been privileged to co-lead three trips with Joel. He leads the adventure, and I lead devotions.

Our inaugural adventure was a four-day hike on the Inca Trail to Machu Picchu. The next year we hiked Half Dome in Yosemite National Park. Last year we spent an epic week rafting the Colorado River and hiking out of the Grand Canyon. And this year I'll go after Life Goal #109. I'll watch the sunrise from the top of Cadillac Mountain in Acadia National Park. And when I do, I'll be the first person in America to see the sunrise that day!

Joel doesn't just lead hiking or rafting trips. Our carefully orchestrated adventures create a field of dreams where people can get a vision from God, not unlike a Native American vision quest.

Because most of us read Scripture in the comfortable confines of air-conditioned homes or offices, we often miss the geographical subplot. The walk from Jerusalem to Jericho is 15.7 miles with a 3,428-foot change in elevation. In other words, the Good Samaritan had to be in good shape. Mount Sinai is 7,487 feet high, which is quite a trek carrying two stone tablets. And the Sea of Galilee is 8.078 miles wide, which is pretty scary if you're in the middle of the lake in a storm.

These facts might seem insignificant to us, but not if you're the one walking it, climbing it, or sailing it. It's no coincidence that Jesus prayed on the beach, fasted in the wilderness, and taught on the mountainside.

I live by a little formula that Joel has adopted for Summit Leaders: *change of pace + change of place = change of perspective.* In other words, geography and spirituality are not unrelated. View affects vision. I think that's why God told Abraham to go outside his tent and look into the night sky.[2] Inside the tent an eight-foot ceiling obstructed his vision. Outside the tent, the sky was the limit.

Not long after surviving Mount Elbrus, Joel picked up a copy of *In a Pit with a Lion on a Snowy Day* and read it in two days. Then he uncharacteristically woke up very early the next morning. "I try to see four o'clock only once per day, and the a.m. version is not the preferred one!" said Joel. "When I'm wide awake at that hour, I pay attention."

Joel heard an inaudible yet unmistakable voice that morning: *It's time to move on the vision. Contact Mark Batterson.* In the wee hours of the morning, Joel typed out his vision for Summit Leaders. Then he made an educated guess at my e-mail address and hit Send. I was in a writing season, so I was up early that day. I saw the e-mail right after Joel sent it. And even though I didn't know Joel from Adam, I e-mailed him back immediately: "I'm all over this idea! Let's talk about what it could look like."

One reason I was all over the idea was that Joel proposed hiking the Inca Trail to Machu Picchu, and that was Life Goal #42. I had just set that goal, and I had a hunch that this was my golden ticket.

Sending that e-mail was a field-of-dreams moment for Joel. And as is often the case with God-ordained dreams, Joel's dream made one of my dreams possible. Because of his obedience to the vision God gave him, I've checked quite a few life goals off my list. And so have lots of other leaders who would rather go on an adventure than go to a conference.

Fight Song

It was an ordinary day in every way, but it was a day that would change the trajectory of my life forever. When the days of my life are measured, it will rank right near the top.

Our family was vacationing at Lake Ida in Alexandria, Minnesota, just as we had done every summer of my life. I was a week away from my sophomore year at the University of Chicago, but my spirit was unsettled. On paper my life was absolutely perfect. I had a full-ride scholarship to one of the top academic institutions in the country and a starting position on the basketball team. But God was stirring the nest, stirring my spirit.

In retrospect I call it my summer of seeking. But at the time I didn't even know what I was looking for. For the first time in my life, prayer was more than punching a timecard. Instead of asking God to bless my plan for Him, I genuinely sought His plan for me—His good, pleasing, and perfect will.

I got up extra early on the last morning of vacation, set out on a prayer walk down a dirt road, and took a shortcut through a cow pasture filled with cow patties. It was in the middle of that cow pasture that I heard the same inaudible yet unmistakable voice of God that Joel heard on Mount Elbrus. It was my burning bush, the place where God came out of nowhere and spoke in a way I'd never heard before.

It's hard to describe, and I don't want to exaggerate what happened. But I knew God was calling me into full-time ministry. I had no idea where or when or how, but I knew I was called to be a pastor.

That cow pasture in Alexandria, Minnesota, is my field of dreams.

It feels like a lifetime ago, but I'm reminded of it almost daily. Nearly a decade ago I took a pilgrimage back to that cow pasture and took pictures. Why? Because there are days when I need to swivel my chair, look at the picture of that decisive moment, and be reminded of why I do what I do.

Your dream is more than a dream. It's a calling. Sure, someone hired you and someone can fire you. But they didn't call you. God did. And if you forget that fact, you forget *why* you do what you do and *Who* you do it for.

Scripture doesn't give much context, but Shammah found himself in a field full of lentils. Why Scripture even nuances that fact, I'm not sure. Lentils were one of the first crops domesticated in the Near East. In other words, this was a farmer's field. But for Shammah, the third-ranked mighty man, it was his battlefield.

We don't know what was going through Shammah's mind, but this was his fight song, take back his life song, prove he's all right song. This was where he took his stand, made his name, and won the greatest battle of his life.

This was Shammah's field of dreams.

Go Back

I love going back to places where God has done something significant in my life. Whenever I have the chance, I revisit the cow pasture in Alexandria, Minnesota. I go back to the chapel balcony in Springfield, Missouri, where I learned to pray, or I drive by the nursing home in Naperville, Illinois, where I preached some of my first sermons. And several times a week I visit the school where I preached my first sermon as the pastor of NCC, because it's now the gym where I work out.

Something about going back to a place where God has proven Himself faithful builds our faith even more. It's not just a walk down memory lane. Those memories fuel faith and stoke the imagination.

I wonder if Shammah ever went back to the field of lentils later in life, the place where he took his stand. I wonder if Abraham ever went back to Mount Moriah, the place where God provided a ram in the thicket. Did Jacob ever double back to the Jabbok River, the place where he wrestled with

God? Did David ever go back to the Valley of Elah, where he defeated Goliath? And what about Elijah? Is it a coincidence that he prayed for rain in the place where God sent fire? I think not. When you go back to a place where God has already done a miracle, you have twice the faith. That's why I climb onto the rooftop of Ebenezers coffeehouse to pray. I have more faith up there!

Before going wherever God wants to take you next, is there some place you need to go back to? Sometimes the way forward is backward. "The farther backward you can look," said Winston Churchill, "the farther forward you can see."[3]

After our first attempt at church planting failed, I thought the dream of planting a church was deep-sixed. I've since discovered that God-ordained dreams often go through a death and resurrection. Only when the dream is dead and buried can it be resurrected for God's glory.

Dreams aren't just born; they are sometimes born again.

Most dreams die not because they're the wrong dream but because the timing is wrong. We're not ready for it, or it isn't ready for us. But what seems like a waiting period is really a grace period. Don't put a period where God puts a comma. When the time is right, dust off the dream and rededicate it to God.

Church planting isn't the only dream that took me two attempts. So did *In a Pit with a Lion on a Snowy Day*. I didn't write the book once; I wrote it twice. It took two attempts to get a contract on the crackhouse that is now Ebenezers coffeehouse. The first contract fell through, and I'm glad it did. God knew we needed another year of financial and numerical growth under our belt before undertaking that project. It felt like a waste of time when it happened, but God's timing is perfect.

More often than not, what we perceive as a *no* is really a *not yet*.

Plan B

My spiritual father, Dick Foth, was a premed student at the University of California, Berkeley, in 1959. During his freshman year he got straight D's in chemistry, so he decided not to inflict himself on the medical community. As Foth likes to say, "No one wants a surgeon who got a D." Foth opted for ministry instead, but it was his plan B.

In 1966 Foth planted a church in Urbana, Illinois, and then pastored it for more than a decade. Then another plan B presented itself when Bethany College in Santa Cruz, California, asked him to interview for their presidency. Dick would serve as president for fourteen years, but he was actually their second choice. It was only after their first choice passed on the job that Dick was offered the job, and by then he was having second thoughts. Maybe because he was their second choice!

When the chairman of the board at Bethany asked Dick to reconsider, he began to pray. He was lying on his bed wrestling with God that day when he heard the still, small voice of the Holy Spirit. The Spirit said something like this: *You know you can pastor, but you aren't sure if you can president. You're afraid of risking your reputation. You're afraid of failing. Aren't you glad I wasn't?*

When we operate in faith, we aren't risking our reputation. We're risking God's reputation! And God can handle Himself just fine, thank you. You may doubt yourself because of your lack of education or lack of experience. But if God has called you, you aren't really doubting yourself. You're doubting God.

God doesn't call the qualified.

God qualifies the called.

My father-in-law, Bob Schmidgall, had at least two dreams that he never fulfilled. He wanted to plant a church in the inner city of Chicago, but it never happened. He also wanted to be a missionary. Instead, he faithfully pastored Calvary Church in Naperville, Illinois, for thirty-one years.

Toward the end of his life, my father-in-law came to terms with his unfulfilled dream of being a missionary. He said to my mother-in-law, "God has used me more by *not* going." And it's true. For many years Calvary Church was the leading mission-giving church in the Assemblies of God. But it's not just the millions of dollars that made a difference. He was a missionary's best friend. And, most important, his heart for missions was passed on to his son Joel and his nephew Dave.

Joel and Dave lead the way at NCC when it comes to missions. This past year we took twenty-eight mission trips and gave more than $2 million to missions. And we're just getting started. We want to *grow more* so we can *give more.* The true measure of a church isn't the seating capacity of its sanctuary. The true measure of spiritual maturity is sending capacity, and we dream of the day when a short-term team is coming and going fifty-two weeks a year. We also dream of the day when the 126 missionaries and ministries we support double and triple and quadruple. We dream of the day when every NCCer is on mission whenever, wherever, whatever.

Sometimes God will put a dream in your heart that is actually for someone else to accomplish. And sometimes there is more joy in watching someone else do it. David dreamed of building a temple, but God said no. God downloaded the plans to David, but it was David's son who would fulfill the dream.

In a similar way I'd like to think that National Community Church is a fulfillment of my father-in-law's dreams. It's located in Washington, DC, rather than Chicago, but I think it still counts. And I know that our vision for missions is a passion within a passion, a dream within a dream.

Planting a church in Chicago was our plan A. I even put together a twenty-five-year plan for a seminary class that got an A, but in reality it earned an F. And I'm so grateful it did fail because that's how we discovered a much better plan, plan B, in Washington, DC.

Don't settle for your plan A.

Go after God's plan B.

Imaginary Drummers

"Oh great! Real bullets!"

"Something amazing, I guess."

"If you build it, he will come."

These one-liners are a few of my film favorites. The first one, from *Three Amigos,* makes me laugh. The second one, from *The Incredibles,* makes me smile. And the third one, from *Field of Dreams,* makes me risk.

In the 1989 classic *Field of Dreams,* Kevin Costner plays the role of novice farmer and baseball lover Ray Kinsella. While walking through a cornfield, Ray hears a faint whisper: "If you build it, he will come." Ray bets the farm by building a baseball diamond in the middle of nowhere. After Kinsella does much soul-searching and penny-pinching, the ghosts of baseball past mysteriously appear and play ball.

That one-liner has become a life metaphor for me.

Many people hit a dead end in their dream journey because they're waiting for God to go first. In my experience signs *follow.*[4] If you wait for God to part the Jordan River, you're going to be waiting the rest of your life. You have to step into the river and get your feet wet before God will part the river.

Faith is taking the first step before God reveals the second step.

When NCC first started, I was both the preacher and worship leader. I didn't lead worship because I was gifted at it. I did it because there wasn't anyone else to do it. I have a heart for worship but not the voice. I don't have the rhythm either!

Our dominant prayer our first year was *Send us a drummer! Save souls too, but send us a drummer!* If I prayed it once, I prayed it a hundred times. One day after praying that prayer, I felt as if God said, *Why don't you buy a drum set?* My reaction? *Just as soon as You send a drummer!* I wanted God to go first. That way there'd be no risk involved. Of course, that also eliminates the element of faith.

This was pre-Google, so I looked for a used drum set in the classifieds. At that point our monthly income as a church was $2,000, and we were paying $1,600 to rent the DC public school where we met, leaving $400 for our salary and all other expenses. You can guess how much the drum set cost, can't you? Four hundred dollars.

I still remember my internal dialogue as I drove to Silver Spring, Maryland, to buy that drum set. *This is crazy! I'm buying a drum set for an imaginary drummer that doesn't even exist.* But it was a field-of-dreams moment—*if you buy it, he will come.* The very next Sunday a clean-shaven young man with a short haircut walked into NCC for the first time. I could tell he was military, but I wasn't sure which branch. Turns out he was stationed at the marine barracks and was with the Drum and Bugle Corps. We have a simple policy at NCC: if you play an instrument for the president of the United States, you don't even have to audition for our worship team! God didn't just send us a drummer; he sent us a rock star. And even more important than the rhythm we added to our worship was the faith that multiplied.

Sometimes you have to take a stand by taking a step. And when you do, that one small step can turn into a giant leap.

Faith Defined

I have quite a few definitions of faith that I've coined and collected over the years. Faith is climbing out on a limb, cutting it off, and watching the tree fall down. If doubt is putting your circumstances between you and God, faith is putting God between you and your circumstances. Faith is unlearning your fears until all that's left is the fear of God. Faith is the willingness to look foolish. And I've already mentioned it, but it's worth repeating: faith is taking the first step before God reveals the second step.

Let me give you one more.

Gratitude is thanking God *after* He does it.

Faith is thanking God *before* He does it.

Sometimes you need to stop praying for something and start praising God as if it has already happened. Isn't that what the Israelites did when they marched around Jericho? God didn't say, "I will deliver it into your hands"—future tense. He said, "I have delivered it"—present perfect tense. In other words, it had already been accomplished in the spiritual realm. All they had to do was circle Jericho until God delivered on His promise.

Dick Eastman is one of my prayer heroes. He's spent more time in prayer than just about anybody I know. Dick made a vow in his twenties to spend an hour with God every day. Now in his seventies, Dick has logged at least sixteen thousand hours in prayer! .

During a recent conversation Dick told me a story about a missionary who was praying for a four-by-four vehicle for their ministry. As a statement of faith, he would wash that imaginary vehicle with soap and water in front of his mission house as very inquisitive African neighbors looked on. That may seem silly to some, but faith often comes across that way. And it's no coincidence that a church in California bought that missionary a four-by-four not long after.

Inspired by his example, Dick did something similar when Every Home for Christ, the organization Dick is president of, was believing God for a building. Dick would often circle the imaginary foundation, open imaginary doors, and walk into his imaginary office. It was Dick's field of dreams. And that dream became reality when EHFC built its headquarters, the Jericho Center, in Colorado Springs, Colorado.

One more story for good measure.

Joshua Symonette is a former Washington Redskin and current campus pastor at National Community Church. His boyhood dream was playing in the NFL, but he was a long shot. Not many NFL teams scouted at Tennessee Technological University, especially since Peyton Manning was playing down the road at the University of Tennessee at the same time as Joshua.

It had been a decade since Tennessee Tech had a player in the NFL, but that only fueled Joshua's fire. Before the start of his sophomore season, he made a decision to wear a suit to every game. Why? Because he noticed that NFL players wore suits to their games. So he followed their example. That may seem insignificant to some, but it was a statement of faith—a dress rehearsal for his dream. If your dream is to play in the pros, why not dress like one?

Now for the fun, or funny, part! Joshua would put on his suit in his dorm room, walk five minutes across an empty campus, and then immediately take off his suit in the locker room. It made no sense to his fellow players or his coaches. But he repeated that ritual, game after game, year in and year out. Why? Because it was his field of dreams.

"If I look ridiculous," Joshua said, "so be it."

That's faith—the willingness to look foolish.

Only one team gave Joshua a shot, but that's all it took. He didn't look ridiculous then! And it's appropriate that he lined up in the same defensive backfield as Hall of Famer Deion Sanders. Why? Because if there was a Suit Hall of Fame, Prime Time would be in on the first ballot! And so would Joshua.

If You Build It

The Bible is full of field-of-dream moments.

If Noah would build the ark, God would send the animals two by two.[5] If Elisha would dig ditches in the desert, God would flood them.[6] If the widow would borrow empty jars, God would fill them with oil.[7]

In 1997 NCC built an ark, dug a ditch, and borrowed jars. We hosted our first Convoy of Hope outreach, which I've already referenced. But that field of dreams moment created a ripple effect.

A decade later we hosted another Convoy of Hope at RFK Stadium, which blessed twice as many people. And it was that outreach that gave birth to the dream for our Dream Center in the nation's capital.

If you want to walk on water, you have to get out of the boat.[8] That first step will feel awfully foolish. But that's how God turns the Sea of Galilee into a field of dreams.

If you want to experience the supernatural, you have to attempt something that is beyond your natural ability. If you want to experience God's miraculous provision, you have to attempt something that is beyond your resources. It might not add up, but God can make it multiply just as it did in a field of dreams filled with five thousand hungry souls two thousand years ago.

One of the first steps in going after your goals is going public. You can announce it to the world via social media, or you can tell a trusted friend. One way or the other, it holds you accountable. And you'll discover that when you put your dream out there, perhaps by putting on a suit and dressing the part, supernatural synchronicities start to happen.

If you build it, He will come.

ON THIS SPOT

At the cave of Adullam
2 Samuel 23:13

THE SKYLINE OF NEW YORK CITY is awe inspiring, to say the least. But what fascinates me even more is the city beneath the city. The city's nine thousand manhole covers service a ninety-eight-thousand-mile labyrinth of utility cables. A six-thousand-mile maze of sewers circulates 1.3 billion gallons of wastewater every day. And there's 722 miles of subway tracks that would stretch all the way to Chicago if laid end to end.

So there's the skyline with its skyscrapers. There's the city beneath the city with its subway. And beneath the city beneath the city there is Manhattan schist, the bedrock that much of New York City is built upon. Like every modern city, the aboveground cityscape mirrors the subterranean topography in more ways than meet the eye.

In 1865 a civil engineer named Egbert Viele published a topographical map that is still used by geotechnical engineers 150 years later. Viele mapped the location of streams, marshes, and coastlines, superimposing them over the street grid. When the sixty-story Chase Manhattan Plaza was built in 1957, the chief engineer failed to reference the Viele Map. If he had, he would have realized that he was building right over a subterranean stream that created quicksand.[1]

Now here's my point.

The brick-and-mortar buildings of New York City stand where there used to be rocks and streams and meadows and forests. If you could reverse the time lapse of the last two hundred years, the concrete jungle would turn back into Central Park. The animals in the Central Park Zoo would still be there, but without the cages.

Just as every *person* has a genealogy, so does every *place*.

Four hundred years ago New York City was New Amsterdam. Its fifteen hundred residents spoke eighteen different languages, because it was a trading outpost for the Dutch West India Company. That layered history makes a place what it is.

What's true of New York City is true of Washington, DC.

It takes a little imagination to picture it in your mind's eye, but the hill where the United States Capitol now stands used to be the epicenter of the Algonquian empire. Instead of museums and street lamps, imagine wigwams and campfires. At the foot of what is now Capitol Hill, there was a council house where all the Algonquian-speaking tribes gathered for important meetings.[2]

It wasn't until the latter half of the seventeenth century that white immigrants settled in the area. On June 5, 1663, a farmer named Francis Pope acquired a four-hundred-acre tract of land that included Jenkins Hill, the hill where the Algonquians had held council. Pope named it Rome. Some thought it was a playful pun, given his last name, but Pope believed it was prophetic. He had a dream that one day a splendid parliament house would be built on the hill now known as Capitol Hill.[3] It was the middle of nowhere two hundred years ago, but Pope was spot on. His pastureland is now the epicenter of the political world.

I once saw a sign that sarcastically said, "On this site in 1897, nothing happened." That's funny! But in reality every geography has a genealogy. Of course, some sites are more storied than others, like the Temple Mount in Jerusalem.

A thousand years before the birth of Christ, it was the threshing floor of Araunah the Jebusite. And a thousand years before that, it was the site on Mount Moriah where God provided a ram in the thicket for Father Abraham.[4] Those events are separated by thousands of years, but they are connected by geography and theology. At the very place where God provided a ram to take Isaac's place, God would provide the Lamb of God to take our place. One event foreshadowed the other by thousands of years.

Just as certain places have incredible historical significance, certain places have incredible personal significance. The cow pasture in Alexandria, Minnesota, where I felt called to ministry is my burning bush. To anyone else it's an ordinary pasture. To me, it's holy ground. For me, it's like the cleft in the rock where Elijah saw God pass by and heard the whisper of God.

That's what the cave of Adullam was for David. It was a dark place, a difficult time. But that's where trust was tempered, where faith was forged. That's where David discovered what it meant to give God the sacrifice of praise.

The cave of Adullam was a thin place—a place where God met David and where David met God in a whole new way. Tough times will do that. The cave of Adullam wasn't where David *wanted* to be, but it's where David *needed* to be for a season. It's there that we discover that the dream isn't about us at all.

The dream is from God.

The dream is for God.

Zoom

On road trips I often pass the time by listening to podcasts. A recent favorite is *Serial,* hosted by Sarah Koenig. The second season of *Serial* details the story of Private First Class Bowe Bergdahl, who goes AWOL from his army base in eastern Afghanistan.

It's a military mystery, which I won't try to unravel. I bring it up only because I love the organizing metaphor that Sarah Koenig uses to thread the storyline. She likens it to *Zoom,* a book she used to read to her children.

Zoom has no words, just pictures. On the first page there is a pointy red shape, but you aren't sure what it is until the next page when you realize it's a rooster's comb. Each page zooms out a little farther. The rooster is standing on a fence with two children watching him. Then you see a farm-house and farm animals, and then you realize that they aren't real. They're actually toys being played with by a child. But wait, the next page reveals that all of it is a scene from an advertisement in a magazine. The magazine is on the lap of someone napping on a deck chair, which is on a cruise ship. With each turn of the page, the aperture gets wider and wider until the original image—a pointy red shape on the rooster's comb—is so far away that it becomes invisible to the naked eye.

"That's what the story of Bowe Bergdahl is like," said Sarah Koenig. "This one idiosyncratic guy makes a radical decision at the age of twenty-three to walk away into Afghanistan, and the consequences of that decision, they spin out wider and wider."[5]

That's true of everyone, of every decision we make. Every decision and every indecision has a ripple effect way beyond our ability to predict. Every cause has an effect, and the effect has a cumulative effect. It also has a hundred unintended consequences that set off a thousand chain reactions.

With that as a backdrop, let me zoom in on the cave of Adullam.

The Proving Ground

It sounds kind of cool, doesn't it? *The cave of Adullam*. Sort of like Wes Anderson's *The Grand Budapest Hotel*. But this was not a five-star resort; it was a last resort. The only reason anyone would ever go there is that there isn't anywhere else to go. This is the last place on earth David wanted to be, but sometimes that is when God has you right where He wants you.

I had a twenty-five-year plan for our church plant in Chicago, but that church plant never got off the ground. I thought the dream was *over*, but Chicago wasn't the final destination; it was a layover. I had the right idea in the wrong place. That failed church plant was God's way of rerouting us to Washington, DC.

The hardest part of any dream journey is the holding pattern.

It's the twenty-five years between God's promise to Abraham and the birth of Isaac. It's the thirteen years between Joseph's dream and his interpretation of Pharaoh's dream. It's the forty years between Moses's dream of delivering Israel and the Exodus.

Almost every dream I've had has gone through some sort of holding pattern, and it can feel like a holding cell. I felt called to write when I was twenty-two, but my first book didn't get published until I turned thirty-five. Thirteen years felt like forever, and I got frustrated. But I leveraged that holding pattern by reading thousands of books while my dream sat on the tarmac.

It took five years of circling a crackhouse in prayer before we finally got a contract on our piece of the promised land. Then it took another five years to rezone 201 F Street NE and build Ebenezers coffeehouse. In the past decade we've served more than a million customers and given more than $1 million in net profits to missions. We've even been voted the number one coffeehouse in DC a time or two. But it took a decade just to get to ground zero.

If you dare to dream big, you better think long.

The day that David was anointed by the prophet Samuel was a day unlike any other, one of the most memorable days of his life. But David didn't become king the next day. David was likely anointed while he was still a teenager, but he didn't become king until the age of thirty. It was a fifteen-year ellipsis that had to feel like forever. But even when David thought the plan wasn't working, God was working His plan.

The cave of Adullam was his proving ground.

Remember when Saul wandered into a cave where David was hiding, and David had him dead to rights? He could have killed Saul and called it self-defense. But David did not dare touch the Lord's anointed. David's band of brothers were ticked off at first, but after the anger wore off, I bet their respect went up a notch or two.

That moment was a microcosm. David forfeited what seemed like a golden opportunity to preserve his integrity. Why? Because an opportunity isn't an opportunity if you have to compromise your integrity. It's the decisions when no one is looking that will dictate your destiny. In fact, your integrity *is* your destiny!

Killing Goliath was an epic act of bravery.

Not killing Saul was an epic act of integrity.

You know how you get a *testimony*? By passing a *test*. No test, no testimony. So count your blessings when you find yourself in the cave of Adullam. The holding pattern is an opportunity to grow, an opportunity to trust, an opportunity to prove your integrity.

Are you in a holding pattern? Make the most of it. Life is lived in seasons, and each season presents unique challenges, unique opportunities.

When I tell people that I used to read more than two hundred books a year in the early years of NCC, some have a hard time believing it. Then I remind them that I pastored a church of twenty-five people. I had time on my hands! I was incredibly frustrated with our growth, or lack thereof. But I made the most of that holding pattern. I now wish I had the time to read like that, but I don't.

Wherever you are, there you are!

Be fruitful right where you're planted.

Genius

The Latin word *genius* had a different connotation in Roman times than it does now. We have individualized the concept and given the label to musical geniuses, fashion geniuses, culinary geniuses. In ancient times it referred to a presiding deity that followed people everywhere they went, like a guardian angel. And there was a second dimension. Not only did every *person* have his or her own unique genius, but so did every *place*.

"Cities, towns, and marketplaces, all possessed their own presiding spirit, a genius loci, that continuously animated them," said Eric Weiner in *The Geography of Genius*.[6] Think Disney, the happiest place on earth; or Silicon Valley, the seedbed of startups; or Nashville, the magnet for country music.

During one of my first classes as a freshman at the University of Chicago, my professor mentioned that we were just a few feet from where Enrico Fermi created the world's first nuclear reactor. I got goose bumps and then hoped it wasn't radiation! The University of Chicago has produced an astounding eighty-nine Nobel Laureates. I never bumped into any of them on campus, but I could feel their presence. There was a genius loci at the U of C, and it's true of every school, every business, every organization.

If you look at Scripture through this filter, it provides an interesting perspective. There are places known for sinfulness, like Sodom and Gomorrah. There are places that seem to be cursed, like Chorazin and Bethsaida. Then there are places where God seems to show up and show off, like Mount Carmel or Mount Sinai.

What does any of that have to do with David?

David's résumé as a warrior-king was impressive. Lots of battles won, lots of kingdoms conquered. But his most enduring legacy may be as a singer-songwriter. His artistic range was impressive, from indie rock to country to R&B. But my favorite album may be David singing the blues. Let's label it *The Cave Sessions*.

The Cave Sessions

There are three tracks recorded in the cave: Psalms 34, 57, and 142. They have a unique vibe, probably because David wrote them during one of the most difficult seasons of his life. That's what makes them so real, so raw. The cave psalms are similar to the prison epistles Paul wrote. The context makes the lyrics so much more powerful. And that's how David made it through this season of his life, by giving God the sacrifice of praise.

We read the psalms through our individualized, westernized point of view, but I bet David's *band* of brothers sang backup. When David sang, "Glorify the LORD with me; let us exalt his name together,"[7] it was David's mighty men who sang harmony.

An old adage says, "Misery loves company." It can be interpreted negatively, but I think it reveals something about our human nature. We can bear just about anything if we don't have to bear it alone.

Like Jonathan, we need an armorbearer to climb the cliff with us.

Like Moses, we need Aaron and Hur to hold up our arms.

Like David, we need mighty men to fight with us and for us.

When you look back on your life as a whole, you'll certainly celebrate the successes. But you'll also take pride in enduring difficult days, overcoming daunting challenges. We dream of winning the crown, like David. But we'll be defined by how we endured disappointment, faced our fears, and learned from our mistakes.

A few years ago I learned a valuable lesson from a two-star general who played a mean guitar on one of our NCC worship teams. He complimented us on how good we were at sharing wins. That's a best practice at NCC. We celebrate what God is doing at the beginning of every staff meeting, and that positivity sets the tone for everything we do.

"You let us share in the miracle," said the general. "But you don't let us share in the struggle." That was a game changer in the way I lead, in the way I preach. When you let people share in the struggle, they have skin in the game. That's how you become a band of brothers, a band of sisters. That's what happened at the cave of Adullam.

The Dream Center

I have a century-old picture of four men in top hats standing in the middle of Pennsylvania Avenue, east of the Anacostia River. What is perhaps the grandest of Pierre Charles L'Enfant's grand avenues was nothing more than a dirt road surrounded by cow pastures. There are only two buildings in the picture. One is a stone firehouse built in 1892. The other is the home of Arthur E. Randle, one of the men pictured, who served as president of the United States Realty Company.

Over the past century the city has grown up around 2909 Pennsylvania Avenue SE. Often referred to as "the forgotten quadrant" of our city, Randle's home sits as a beacon of hope in one of the most crime-ridden, poverty-stricken parts of our city. Two decades ago it was dubbed the Southeast White House because its architecture resembles that of the White House, plus it sits on Pennsylvania Avenue. A house on the hill for all people, the Southeast White House is a place where children from Randle Highlands

School are mentored, a place where reconciliation lunches bridge the racial divide, a place where hospitality happens in the name of Jesus.

That's the short story, but let me share the struggle.

Remember the Convoy of Hope that we hosted at RFK Stadium? It was a banner day for NCC as we pulled off an outreach that touched ten thousand people. After the outreach we were patting ourselves on the back. That's when we felt as if the Holy Spirit said, *Now I want you to do this every day.*

Every day? It took a year of planning to pull off that one day. It also took eighty-five churches and nonprofits. The thought of doing something like that every day seemed impossible, but we started dreaming about a Dream Center.

For five years we looked for a footprint, a place where we could have a presence in one of the most underprivileged, underresourced parts of our city. Every avenue we pursued proved to be a dead end. What we didn't know was that the answer was right under our nose.

The Southeast White House started the same year we started pastoring NCC—1996. And over the years we had cultivated a friendship, a partnership. We knew we didn't need a building to make a difference, so we started recruiting NCCers to serve as mentors at the Southeast White House. Then we started hosting the reconciliation lunch. Then we purchased the abandoned apartment building next to the Southeast White House, which was transformed into our DC Dream Center this year.

I won't bore you with the details, but it's taken about a decade to get to ground zero. But when your dream has eternal objectives, it gives you the patience to think long. We want to do things that make a difference a hundred years from now, so a decade is a drop in the bucket.

By definition a God-sized dream is bigger than you are. You don't have the time, talent, or treasure to pull it off. Without divine intervention it's destined to fail. But here's what I've found: if you keep growing, what is impossible today can be accomplished in a year or two or ten. Of course, it will probably involve some cave sessions along the way!

In our first year as a church, our total income was less than $50,000.

Fast-forward twenty years. Our giving on the last day of last year was five times that. In other words, God provided *five times as much* in *one day* as He did in *one year* twenty years ago! That's how faith and faithfulness work.

When God does a miracle, you believe Him for bigger and better miracles the next time. That's how you steward miracles—you up the ante. You keep leapfrogging by faith until one day you look back and can hardly believe how far you've come with God's help. That's how David must have felt when he finally found himself on the throne of Israel. But I bet he wouldn't trade the cave sessions for anything. The lessons learned were too valuable.

If you're in the cave of Adullam, give God the sacrifice of praise. It's an opportunity to prove your integrity. Let God write music in you, through you. If you stay patient and persistent, God is going to come through for you. You'll look back on this season with fond memories because they forged faith in you.

So keep on keeping on.

The best is yet to come.

THE LION'S DEN

Is it not the blood of men who went at the risk of their lives?

2 Samuel 23:17

WITH HIS HANDS TIED behind his back, J. W. Tucker was brutally beaten with broken bottles. After torturing Tucker and sixty of his Christian compatriots, their captors threw them into the crocodile-infested Bomokande River to be eaten alive. It wasn't ISIS or Al-Qaeda who claimed responsibility. The attack took place on November 24, 1964, at the hands of Congolese rebels.

Our natural instinct is to feel sorry for Tucker, whose earthly life was seemingly cut short. But life can't be cut short when it lasts for all eternity. A holy empathy for his wife and children, who survived the terrorist attack, is biblically mandated. Angeline lost a husband. Johnny, Carol, and Melvin lost a father. But heaven gained a hero, a hero in a long line of heroes who trace their genealogy back to the first Christian martyr, Stephen. And if we could covet in heaven, we would covet the martyr's reward.

In the grand scheme of God's good, pleasing, and perfect will, eternal gain infinitely offsets earthly pain. God doesn't promise us happily ever after. He promises so much more than that—happily *forever* after.

It was that eternal perspective that inspired J. W. Tucker to risk his earthly life for the gospel. Tucker didn't fear death because he had already died to self.

It wasn't an uncalculated risk that led J. W. Tucker into the Congo during a civil war. He counted the cost with his missionary friend Morris Plotts. Plotts tried to convince his friend not to go. "If you go in," he prophetically pleaded, "you won't come out." To which Tucker responded, "God didn't tell me I had to come out. He only told me I had to go in."[1]

Can't you hear Benaiah saying the exact same thing?

Chasing a five-hundred-pound lion demands complete consecration. It's not *Win, Lose, or Draw.* It's life or death—no escape plan, no backup plan. We celebrate Benaiah because he came out of the lion's den alive, and that's an amazing feat, but it's not the most amazing part of the story. It's not *coming out* that is courageous; it's *going in.*

It's not about coming out with an album; it's about going into the recording studio and laying down tracks. It's not about coming out with a loan; it's about going into the bank with a bang-up business plan. It's not about coming out with a sale; it's about going into the meeting with a perfect pitch. It's not about coming out with a book deal; it's about going into the publisher's office with the best manuscript possible.

Success Defined

We live in a culture that idolizes success and demonizes failure. But in God's kingdom the outcome isn't the issue. Success isn't winning or losing; it's obeying. It's honoring God whether you're in the red or the black. It's praising God whether you win the election or lose it. It's giving God the glory whether you're in the win column or the loss column.

I've never met anybody who doesn't want to be successful, but very few people have actually defined success for themselves. So by default they buy into the culture's definition of success instead of God's definition. In God's book success is spelled *stewardship.* It's making the most of the time, talent, and treasure God has given you. It's doing the best you can with what you have where you are.

Here's my personal definition of success: when those who know you best respect you most. Success starts with those who are closest to you. At the end of the day, I want to be famous in my home.[2] And by the way, it's hard to be famous in your home if you're never home.

If you succeed at the wrong thing, you've failed.

If you fail at the right thing, you've succeeded.

A few years ago I was on vacation at Lake Anna, a hundred miles southwest of Washington, DC. I walked into a little coffee shop and noticed a piece of wall art that said "Chase the Lion." Turns out the owner was inspired to quit her job and pursue her dream of opening Not Just Mochas after reading *In a Pit*. I popped in every time I was in the area, but the shop closed down less than two years after it opened. Not only did I miss the caramel macchiato with a shot of cinnamon, but I also felt partially responsible. However, in my eyes Linda didn't fail. Her dream was *going into* business, and she did just that. Going out of business wasn't part of the plan, but she is no less a lion chaser because the shop closed.

Just as courage is not the absence of fear, success is not the absence of failure. Failure is a necessary step in every dream journey. I've written books that have been disappointments, and I've started businesses that have gone belly up. But in each instance I've tried to learn the lessons those failures are trying to teach me. Then I've mustered the courage to try, try, and try again.

If you don't try out, you'll miss out. Then you'll have to live the rest of your life wondering, *What if?* Don't let the fear of failing keep you from trying.

Given our locale in Washington, DC, I pastor to a lot of professional politicians. Outside the beltway there is a great deal of skepticism toward politicians, and much of it is merited. But public service in the form of politics is a noble profession, even if every politician isn't. The way I see it, running for political office is chasing a five-hundred-pound lion. I've met some politicians who have run and won, but I might admire those who have run and lost even more. They might not have won the popular vote, but they threw their hat into the ring.

God doesn't always call us to win.

Sometimes He just calls us to try.

Either way, it's obedience that glorifies God.

You Like That

During the 2015 NFL season, Kirk Cousins broke almost every Washington Redskins' passing record on the books. He also led the Skins to the largest comeback in their storied eighty-three-year history. The Redskins were trailing the Tampa Bay Buccaneers by twenty-four points in the third quarter when Kirk tied a single-game record with thirty-three completions. His 317 yards, three touchdowns, and 124.7 rating were enough to get the W on a last-second touchdown pass to tight end Jordan Reed.

On the way into the locker room, Kirk yelled, "You like that!"

Redskins fans have been chanting it ever since.

Before his senior season at Michigan State, Kirk's mom gave him a copy of *In a Pit with a Lion on a Snowy Day*. And Kirk was reading it right before one of the biggest games of the season. The Big Ten championship was on the line, and Kirk was as anxious as he'd ever been before a football game.

> When we arrived at Penn State—home of the Nittany *Lions*—it was snowing. And their stadium, with its steep sides and field built deep into the ground, feels just like a pit. I thought, *how fitting . . . in a pit, with a lion, on a snowy day.*[3]

I can only imagine the adrenaline that surged through Benaiah's veins when he faced off against a giant Egyptian and went toe-to-toe with two lionlike Moabites. But they were men, which means Benaiah could guess and second-guess how they would punch and counterpunch. But a lion? Far more unpredictable! And unpredictability produces high levels of anxiety. Benaiah was probably as nervous as he'd ever been, but he channeled his adrenaline.

That's what Kirk did, despite the 108,000 Lions' fans cheering *against* him.

Right before running out of the tunnel, Coach Mark Dantonio threw out a question to his team: "Does anybody know what Psalm 91 says?" His quarterback knew the answer: "You will trample lions." With that, the team prayed and then played their way to a twenty-eight to twenty-two victory and a piece of the Big Ten title.

If you follow professional football, you know that Kirk's journey has been anything but a forty-five degree angle to success. He wasn't drafted in the first round. He rode the bench his first season. Kirk has had his fair share of ups and downs. But when others give up, lion chasers step up. When they experience a setback, they know that God has already prepared their comeback.

After games Kirk and his wife, Julie, have been known to pop into Ebenezers coffeehouse. Kirk is the same person after a loss as he is after a win. He knows that success is about more than winning or losing a football game.

It's how you handle adversity.

It's how you handle disappointment.

It's how you handle mistakes.

It's how you handle an offense.

Those things will make you bitter or better. And the answer is up to you. Even if it isn't your fault, you can take response-ability.

Don't let it steal your joy.

Let it fuel your fire!

The goal isn't winning. The goal is God's glory. And that isn't contingent upon the final score. That *is* the final score!

Amazing Is on the Way

One of my annual rituals is coming up with a word for the year and a verse for the year. This year the word is *consecration*. And the verse is Joshua 3:5: "Consecrate yourselves, for tomorrow the LORD will do amazing things among you."

When I speak to leaders, I sometimes ask, "Who wants to do something amazing for God?" Every hand goes up every time! Then I apologize for the trick question. We all want to do something amazing for God, but that isn't our job. That's God's job! Our job is to consecrate ourselves. And if we do our job—if we go all in and all out, day in and day out—God is going to show up and show off.

Consecrate yourself today, and amazing is on the way!

That sounds great, doesn't it? But one of the hardest things to trust God with is the outcome. That's true whether you're running a campaign, running a business, or running a race. What God cares about most is *not* the polling numbers, the quarterly earnings, or the winning time.

We live in a culture where many people base self-worth on net worth, but in God's kingdom they are statistically unrelated. Our reward directly correlates to the motives of our heart. If you do the right thing for the wrong reason, it doesn't count. So it's not about your voting record, business record, or win-loss record. It's about doing the right things for the right reasons.

The key to pursuing your dream is doing it for intrinsic reasons. In other words, it can't be about fame or fortune. The will of God is not wealth, health, and prosperity. It's not even winning. The will of God is the glory of God.

The eleventh chapter of Hebrews is one of the most amazing chapters in the Bible. It's an unparalleled celebration of faith. But it's also a definition of success. And the definition is somewhat surprising:

> I do not have time to tell about Gideon, Barak, Samson and Jephthah, about David and Samuel and the prophets, who through faith conquered kingdoms, administered justice, and gained what was promised; who shut the mouths of lions, quenched the fury of the flames, and escaped the edge of the sword.[4]

So far so good, right? "All's well that ends well," to quote Shakespeare. But unfortunately the chapter doesn't end there. Here's the rest of the story:

> There were others who were tortured, refusing to be released so that they might gain an even better resurrection. Some faced jeers and

flogging, and even chains and imprisonment. They were put to death by stoning; they were sawed in two; they were killed by the sword.[5]

Here's my question: Were only half of these heroes in the will of God? The ones who conquered kingdoms, quenched flames, and shut the mouths of lions? Or was the other half in the will of God as well, including those who were sawed in two?

The will of God is not an insurance plan.

The will of God is a dangerous plan.

The will of God might get you killed. But if God gets the glory, goal accomplished. And the eternal reward we receive will infinitely outweigh the temporal sacrifice we make.

The Lion's Den

Two days after J. W. Tucker's death, Belgian paratroopers rescued the rest of the family. An Air Force C130 turboprop airlifted them back to America. Angeline's heart was grieved beyond words, but she gave God the sacrifice of praise. She prayed this prayer at twenty thousand feet:

> O, Father, we do thank Thee for Thy goodness and love and many blessings. We love Thee and praise Thee for Thy care. And through these many difficult days Thou hast watched over us and kept us. And now Thou hast truly delivered us out of the lion's den. We praise Thee and thank Thee for it. And we ask that you take J's life, which has been laid down, and use it in death for Thine honor and glory.[6]

For thirty years it seemed like J. W. Tucker's sacrifice was all for naught. But God answered his widow's prayer in a unique way.

The Bomokande River flows through the middle of an unreached people group called the Mangbetu tribe. During a time of civil unrest, the

Mangbetu king appealed to his government for help. They sent a man known as the Brigadier, a policeman that J. W. Tucker had led to the Lord two months before he was killed. His efforts to share the gospel with the Mangbetu failed until he discovered an ancient tribal tradition: *If the blood of any man flows in the Bomokande River, you must listen to his message.* The Brigadier gathered the village elders and told them of a man whose blood flowed in the river.

> Some time ago a man was killed, and his body was thrown into your Bomokande River. The crocodiles in this river ate him up. His blood flowed in your river. But before he died, he left me a message. This message concerns God's Son, the Lord Jesus Christ, who came to this world to save people who were sinners. He died for the sins of the world; He died for my sins. I received this message, and it changed my life.[7]

Several members of the tribe fell on their knees, surrendering their lives to the lordship of Jesus Christ. Since that day thousands of Mangbetu have come to faith in Christ, and there are dozens of churches in that region because of the man whose blood flowed in the Bomokande River.

It's not for naught.

It never is!

Every prayer will be answered, every sacrifice will be honored, every good deed will be rewarded, and every seed of faith will bear fruit.

FIGHT CLUB

A valiant fighter from Kabzeel

2 Samuel 23:20

I SHOT A TOMMY GUN at the FBI headquarters. Well, not *at it,* in it. Special agents Zac Jury and Matt Heimstra not only gave our campus pastors a private tour, but they also let me shoot an original 1918 John T. Thompson submachine gun in the FBI shooting range. I was warned that the Tommy gun has quite a kick when it's set on fully automatic. Let's just say I left my mark on the FBI that day. By the time I emptied the magazine, the ceiling of the shooting range had dozens of bullet holes, and cement dust blanketed the range.

Zac Jury was teaching high school history on September 11, 2001. After the first plane hit the Twin Towers, Zac turned on the television in his classroom. When the second plane hit, one of his students started sobbing and said, "Mr. Jury, my sister works in those buildings." That was a genesis moment for Zac, the moment he determined in his heart to devote his life to counterterrorism and pursue his dream of working for the Federal Bureau of Investigation.

Like Josheb, Zac faced long odds.

In fact, his odds were longer than eight hundred to one.

Only 3 percent of applicants who take the Phase I test get invited to take the Phase II test, and only 1.5 percent of those who pass Phase II make it through the FBI background check and graduate from the FBI Academy. But those odds didn't keep Zac from taking a step of faith and quitting his teaching job. "The night before the last day of school," Zac said, "as I was writing my resignation letter, I got a call that I was accepted for the Phase II test."

When Zac arrived at the FBI Academy in Quantico, Virginia, he felt like he was out of his league. "There were former military special forces, scientists, lawyers, police officers, and me—just a teacher," Zac said. "Then I remembered that the Lord is the One who had brought me here, so I must belong here."

On the second day at the academy, trainees are shown the photos of every FBI special agent who has been killed in the line of duty. It's a psychological test of sorts, and some don't make it past day two. During the twenty-one weeks, they take fitness tests, legal tests, firearms tests, and defensive tactics tests.

The final test is called Bull in the Ring. It's a no-holds-barred, knock-down-drag-out fight. Weighing in at 185 pounds, Zac was put in the heavyweight group, ranging from 180 to 220 pounds. He also had two Golden Gloves boxers in his group, but he held his own.

"Most people have never been in a fight in their life," Zac said. "This one exercise gives you confidence the rest of your career that if you ever get in a fight, it is going to be a fight for your life."

Bull in the Ring

"A valiant fighter."

We read right past it, but it's everything I need to know about Benaiah. He was a valiant fighter. Instead of Bull in the Ring, Benaiah survived Lion in a Pit.

Benaiah would have impressed at the NFL Combine. He was well conditioned and well trained. But this descriptor reveals more about Benaiah's moral character than it does his physical prowess.

According to rabbinic tradition, when the queen of Sheba came to visit Solomon, he sent Benaiah to meet her. Benaiah was described as "the hind at dawn leaping into the sunlight."[1] An ancient compliment, I guess. The queen of Sheba actually descended from her chariot, mistaking him for

King Solomon. When the queen discovered her error, she quoted an appropriate proverb: "You have not yet seen the lion, come and behold his den."[2]

Benaiah may not have been "the lion king," but he was the lion chaser!

Fighters don't walk away when the going gets tough; they fight to the finish for their convictions. Fighters don't give up when everyone is against them; they fight against the status quo. And fighters don't shrink back when the odds are against them; they fight back for what they believe in.

There is a moment in every dream journey when you have to fight for what you believe in. It might be a marriage that is on the ropes, a child who is in rebellion, or a dream that is on life support.

Are you willing to fight for it?

There is only one way to get out of a pit with a lion on a snowy day— you have to fight your way out. You have to fight harder, fight longer, and fight smarter than your five-hundred-pound foe.

According to the tale of the tape, Benaiah was a serious underdog. In the world of prize fighting, reach is everything. The giant Egyptian that Benaiah faced off against stood seven feet six inches tall.[3] So Benaiah's chances of defeating this giant were about the same as David's chances of defeating Goliath! But the old adage is true: it's not the size of the dog in the fight; it's the size of the fight in the dog.

I'm laid-back about almost everything, but don't mess with my family or my dream. If you mess with either of them, you mess with me. A protective instinct takes over, and I'll take you down.

Are you willing to fight for your dream?

To fight until your hand freezes to the sword?

To fight even if it's eight hundred against one?

Six Rounds

I was speaking at a leadership conference in Dallas, Texas, on March 24, 2015. Two minutes before going on stage, my phone rang. Usually I wouldn't answer it, but I recognized the number. That's how I discovered that my dad had cancer. Needless to say, it was one of the toughest talks I've ever given. While I was talking, I was processing the questions that started firing across my synapses.

What kind is it?

What stage is it?

What are the chances of beating it?

Some people roll over and play dead when backed into a corner by bad news, but my dad isn't wired that way. Even when we discovered that the cancer was in two places, my dad came out of the corner fighting with an upbeat attitude. I don't have a single memory of my dad complaining about anything, and cancer wasn't about to change his approach to life! My dad fought cancer the way he has fought every other challenge—with grace and faith. And we fought for him in prayer.

The Enemy comes to steal your joy, kill your dreams, and destroy your life. Jesus came that you might have life and have it more abundantly. Simply put, we were born on a battlefield between good and evil, and we have to choose sides. I'm not one of those people who see a demon behind every bush. But I also know that our struggle is not against flesh and blood. We're in a dogfight with the devil, and we don't have to take it sitting down.

No weapon formed against us will prosper.[4]

If we resist the devil, he will flee from us.[5]

And if God is for us, who can be against us?[6]

The Bible says the devil prowls around like a roaring lion. The key word is *like*. He's a poser, and his bark is worse than his bite. Refuse to believe his lies or to cower to his intimidation. When he reminds you of your past, remind him of his future!

Fight back with words of faith.

Fight back with songs of praise.

Complex Trauma

Bonnie Martin is a licensed professional counselor with expertise in complex trauma. Her job is helping the victims of violence, exploitation, and human trafficking get out of the nightmare they find themselves in. Bonnie is also a former English teacher and the one who edited the first draft of *In a Pit with a Lion on a Snowy Day* ten years ago!

One of the defining moments of her life occurred during a very difficult season. In the height of her ministry career, her marriage was failing. Despair was closing in on her like a dense fog. Bonnie went on a mission trip to South Africa with her father just to escape her painful situation for a little while. On the last day there, they went on a safari and came within two feet of a lion. Separated from it by a chain-link fence, Bonnie playfully said, "Hey kitty, kitty!" That's when the lion lunged at the fence and let out a roar that still makes her shudder a decade later!

"My nerves caught fire," said Bonnie. "It felt like death by electrocution."

Bonnie learned from her guide that a lion's roar is meant to communicate dominance—to assert its authority in a territory. And the only thing that will silence a lion's roar is the roar of a more powerful lion.

That's when Bonnie heard the still, small voice of the Holy Spirit:

Bonnie, Satan walks around like a roaring lion looking to devour. But do you see that fence? That fence is the blood of Jesus, the blood of the Lamb. Satan may roar at you, but he cannot touch you. He is the one in a cage. You are the one that's free. But you have been living your life like you're the one in the cage and he is the one that's free.

Come on!

Greater is He that is in you than he that is in the world![7]

Bonnie's circumstances didn't change that day, but her perspective did. The darkness actually got darker. The pit got deeper. But in the words of Corrie ten Boom, "There is no pit that God's love is not deeper still."[8] Bonnie's first marriage ended, but a new chapter in her life began.

Instead of seeing herself as a victim, Bonnie saw herself for who she is—more than a conqueror. She leveraged her pain by getting licensed as a professional counselor, and she is helping women all around the world find and fight their way out of whatever pit they find themselves in.

When the Lion of the tribe of Judah roared His way out of the tomb on the third day, He didn't just defeat death. He asserted His authority over His ancient foe, silencing sin once and for all. Satan is a defeated foe.

It's okay to talk to God about your problems, but at some point you need to talk to your problems about God.

Preach the goodness of God to them. Prophesy the promises of God to them. Proclaim the victory that was won two thousand years ago!

Jesus rebuked the wind and the waves. He rebuked demons. He even rebuked a fever. So I think it's okay to rebuke cancer. I can't promise healing, but I can pray for it. And I know that our healing, our deliverance was paid in full at Calvary's cross.

My dad went six rounds with chemo, and he walked away with a clean bill of health. He has a few battle scars for sure, but he fought a good fight. I love my dad even more after his fight against cancer because I know he wasn't fighting just for himself. He was fighting for my mom, fighting for me and my brother, fighting for his six grandchildren.

Whatever challenge you face, don't take it sitting down.

Pick a fight with injustice.

Pick a fight with poverty.

Pick a fight with racism.

If you're willing to fight for it, you have a fighting chance. And God will fight for you.

Valor

During our tour of FBI headquarters, we paused in front of a plaque with the names of every FBI agent who has received the Medal of Valor. It's awarded to those who have shown exceptional heroism in the line of duty. On the plaque is a quote by Pulitzer Prize–winning poet Carl Sandburg.

Valor is a gift. Those having it never know for sure whether they have it till the test comes. And those having it in one test never know for sure if they will have it when the next test comes.

Valor is less an action and more a reaction.

If you judge a person by his or her actions, you're judging a book by its cover. Reactions are far more revealing than actions. How you react in difficult circumstances is the litmus test of character. And you never really know how you'll react until you're the one who crosses paths with a lion.

Valor is running toward trouble when everyone else is running away.

Valor is going above and beyond the call of duty.

Valor is putting yourself in the line of fire for someone else.

Putting oneself in harm's way is counterintuitive to the average person, but it's second nature to a lion chaser. As King David's bodyguard, that was Benaiah's job description. He had been trained how to make his body the largest possible target, step in front of the king, and take a spear if need be.

Transformed Nonconformist

Shortly after being installed as the twentieth pastor of Dexter Avenue Baptist Church in Montgomery, Alabama, Dr. Martin Luther King Jr. delivered a sermon in November of 1954 titled "Transformed Nonconformist."

"The Christian is called upon not to be like a thermometer conforming to the temperature of his society," said King, "but he must be like a thermostat serving to transform the temperature of his society."[9]

King recognized that being different for difference's sake isn't the goal. The goal is to make a difference. And that takes the courage not just to stand but to stand alone.

"I have seen many white people who sincerely oppose segregation and [discrimination]," said King. "But they never took a [real] stand against it because of fear of standing alone."[10]

Are you willing not just to stand but to stand alone?

On December 1, 1955, a transformed nonconformist boarded the Cleveland Avenue bus just five blocks from the pulpit where King delivered that sermon. When the white section filled up with passengers, the bus driver ordered Rosa Parks to give up her seat in the colored section. Rosa politely refused. She took a moral stand by remaining seated.

"People always say that I didn't give up my seat because I was tired, but that isn't true," Rosa said.[11] It wasn't a physical tiredness that kept Rosa seated; it was a moral tiredness. "The only tired I was, was tired of giving in."[12]

Rosa Park's stand against racial segregation started a ripple effect. It led to a court battle, which led to a citywide boycott, which led to the Supreme Court ruling segregation unconstitutional.

Until the pain of staying the same becomes more acute than the pain of change, nothing happens. We simply maintain the status quo. And we convince ourselves that playing it safe is safe. But the greatest risk is taking no risks at all.

Wouldn't Be Prudent

"Not gonna do it. Wouldn't be prudent."

It's a classic catch phrase made famous by Dana Carvey's impersonation of President George H. W. Bush on *Saturday Night Live*. I hear Dana Carvey's voice when I read about Benaiah's exploits.

Chase a lion? "Not gonna do it. Wouldn't be prudent."

Take on two mighty Moabites? "Not gonna do it. Wouldn't be prudent."

Fight a giant Egyptian? "Not gonna do it. Wouldn't be prudent."

None of these actions seems prudent, but that's what makes them valiant. I'm all for doing homework. I believe due diligence honors God, but delayed obedience disguised as prudence is disobedience. And it won't get you where God wants you to go.

For more than forty years, Dr. Glen Reid served as a missionary in the

Middle East. Everyone who knew him had the utmost respect for him. So they were surprised by his courageous confession at the age of eighty-two: "I have failed throughout my life because I have let fear and prudence be my gods while I avoided trusting God."

Dr. Reid shared about a moment on the mission field when God prompted him to share the gospel with a tribe of cannibals. Dr. Reid decided not to chase that lion. His excuse was prudence, and it ranks as one of his great regrets. Later in life he recognized prudence for what it really was, his god.

Quit bowing down to the god of prudence!

Faith isn't logical or illogical; it's theological.

Faith isn't prudent or imprudent; it's valiant.

Noah looked foolish building an ark in the desert. Sarah looked foolish buying maternity clothes at age ninety. David looked foolish attacking Goliath with a slingshot. Benaiah looked foolish chasing a lion. The wise men looked foolish following a star. Peter looked foolish stepping out of the boat in the middle of the Sea of Galilee. And Jesus looked foolish hanging half-naked on the cross.

But that's faith. Faith is the willingness to look foolish. And the results speak for themselves.

Noah survived the Great Flood. Sarah gave birth to Isaac. David defeated Goliath. Benaiah killed a lion in a pit on a snowy day. The wise men found the Messiah. Peter walked on water. And Jesus rose from the dead.

You know why some of us have never killed a giant, chased a lion, or walked on water? We're afraid of looking foolish.

But it's the fear of looking foolish that is foolish!

Not Gonna Happen

Before getting married twenty years ago, Jeffrey Keafle and his fiancée, Sherri, outlined their goals for family, finances, and the future. With regard to the future, Jeffrey dreamed big. He told Sherri that he wanted to manage two golf courses—Bellerive Country Club in her hometown of St. Louis, Missouri, and Congressional Country Club in Bethesda, Maryland.

With seventeen thousand golf courses in America, to specify two by name equates to a 1 in 289 million chance of success! It didn't help the odds that they are both top-rated courses. Jeffrey wasn't chasing one five-hundred-pound lion; he was chasing two!

Twelve years later Jeffrey landed one of those dream jobs as chief executive of Bellerive. And that's when he decided to dream even bigger! What if they could host a major championship—and not just any championship but a centennial? Major golf championships have migrated to highly populated East and West Coast courses. And with complex event staging and broadcast requirements, tournaments typically choose multiple-course facilities. Bellerive didn't fit either profile, but that didn't stop Jeffrey from forming a dream team and writing an eighty-page proposal outlining a vision for the future of championship golf.

The championship committee told Jeffrey it was an impressive presentation but Bellerive was not getting a major. In other words, *not gonna happen*.

Jeffrey flew back to St. Louis discouraged, but waiting for him was a copy of *In a Pit with a Lion on a Snowy Day*, a Christmas gift from his golf professional. The question on the back cover immediately caught his attention:

> What if the life you really want, and the future God wants for you,
> is hiding right now in your biggest problem, your worst failure, your
> greatest fear?

Jeffrey decided not to take no for an answer. Despite spending hundreds of hours on the original proposal, he expanded the team working on the project and spent more time revising his proposal, making it even bolder. The committee was intrigued enough with the updated proposal that they asked him to "put more fabric to it."

Two versions later the dream of championship golf benefiting the local community became the genesis of PGA REACH—Recreation, Education, Awareness, Community, and Health. Bellerive beat the odds! It will play host to the one hundredth PGA Championship in 2018. Even more important, its members and the PGA Gateway Section are now positively influencing the lives of disadvantaged youth in the inner city of St. Louis.

I met Jeffrey after he had chased his second lion to Bethesda, Maryland, accepting the CEO position at Congressional Country Club. As we talked over coffee, I saw in him what I see in all lion chasers. Impossible odds don't break their spirit. Impossible odds steel their resolve and fuel their fire. Lion chasers have a sanctified stubborn streak that refuses to give up when they can fight for their God-given dreams.

Play Offense

Let me induct one more member into the fight club.

Gary Cook has been a university president for twenty-eight years. That's a long tenure, but it was almost cut short when Gary was diagnosed with acute leukemia at age fifty-seven. Some people would start living defensively at that point, but not Gary. Gary asked God for another ten thousand days! Why? Because God had given him a $100 million dream!

When you've been the president of a university for twenty-eight years, it's tough to give it up. But God had given Gary a new dream of raising $100 million in scholarships for future students. As he wrestled with his decision, he read my book *Wild Goose Chase*.

The day before the board meeting where he planned to declare his dream, his decision, Gary was wavering. That's when he got to page 66:

If you aren't willing to throw down your staff, you forfeit the miracle that is at your fingertips. You have to be willing to let go of an old identity in order to take on a new identity. . . .

Where do you find your identity? What is the source of your

security? Is it a title? a paycheck? a relationship? a degree? a name? There is nothing wrong with any of those things as long as you can throw them down.[13]

It was a page 66 vision!

When Gary read those words, the decision was made. He put his twenty-eight-year presidency on the altar, believing the best was yet to come. He's devoting the rest of his days to the $100 million dream God has given him.

One fun footnote.

Gary also read *In a Pit with a Lion on a Snowy Day* after his bout with leukemia, and he read it quite literally. He reckoned that the mighty men were *mighty*, so Gary started working out one hour every day. He started getting the sleep, eating the food, and drinking the water he needed to whip his body back into shape. I daresay that Gary is in better shape at sixty-five than most people half his age!

"So many people go on defense at sixty-five," Gary said. "I decided to play offense."

That's what lion chasers do! They play offense with their lives.

RUN TO THE ROAR

He chased a lion.

2 Samuel 23:20, NLT

IT RANKS AS ONE OF THE most unforgettable days of my life. There are days, and then there are days that redefine every day thereafter. May 27, 2005, is one of those days.

I was part of a mission team from National Community Church that spent a week in Ethiopia caring for the poor and serving street children. We even built a mud hut for an elderly Ethiopian grandmother. After we had fulfilled our mission, our friends took us on an unforgettable trip to Awash National Park in the Ethiopian outback.

A few hours outside of Addis Ababa, our caravan stopped for a picnic lunch. We spotted some cows grazing nearby, and because cows in other countries are far more fascinating than American cows, we snapped some pictures. That's when armed shepherds carrying AK-47s ran toward us, yelling in Amharic. Come to find out, if you take pictures of their cows, they want some cash. Their cows are *cash* cows!

Have you ever had an experience that was absolutely terrifying in the moment, but the split second it was over, it was *completely awesome?* This was one of those! And it wasn't even noon yet.

A few hours after being held at gunpoint, we went off-road and drove into a place that could have passed for the Garden of Eden. Hidden in the dense foliage was a natural spring heated by a volcano. According to our guides it was 114 degrees, and I believe them. We weren't in the water five minutes when one of the guys on our team fainted. Fortunately we caught the whole thing on camera so we could replay the fainting episode—I mean rescue operation—over and over again.

Finally we arrived at Awash National Park, climbed onto Land Rovers, and did a game drive as the African sun set. I'm a fan of zoos, but there is nothing like seeing wild animals in their natural habitat, especially when you don't even know the names of half the animals you're seeing!

That evening we set up our camp in a site that was inhabited by at least eighty baboons. Have you ever seen a baboon's butt? Don't tell me God doesn't have a sense of humor! One of the greatest moments of the day was watching someone on our team get pooped on by a baboon perched up in a tree. Not even kidding! That person has since forgiven me for laughing out loud.

At the end of this unforgettable day, we sat around a bonfire singing worship choruses. It was one of those moments when you can't *not* worship. Then one of our armed guards gestured for us to be quiet. That's when we heard a lion roaring, we hoped in the distance! In a word, it was awesome. And by *awesome* I mean exhilarating and frightening. It's very different hearing a lion's roar in the wild from hearing it at the beginning of an MGM film.

Imagine the chill that went down Benaiah's spine when that lion roared. A lion's roar can be heard five miles away! What's it like hearing it and feeling it from two feet away? The natural reaction is to run in the opposite direction or shrink into a fetal position. But Benaiah did not operate in the spirit of timidity. Instead of letting fear dictate his decision, he made one of the most courageous and counterintuitive decisions in all of Scripture.

It was a day that redefined every one of his days thereafter.

When you've chased a lion into a pit on a snowy day, not much scares you after that. And that goes for the rest of David's mighty men.

For Josheb-Basshebeth it was the day he raised his spear against eight hundred men. For Eleazar it was the day his hand froze to his sword. For Shammah it was the day he took his stand in his field of dreams.

Choose Adventure

As I got into my pup tent at the end of that most memorable day, I tried to savor every moment by capturing it in my journal. That's when I heard the still, small voice of the Holy Spirit: *Don't accumulate possessions; accumulate experiences.* That mantra has redefined the way I live my life. It has shaped every day from that day to this. When given a choice, I choose adventure!

It's more than a narrative; it's a metanarrative.

It's more than a story; it's a storyline.

Are you living your life in a way that is worth telling stories about?

The sad reality is that most people spend their lives accumulating the wrong things. Instead of accumulating experiences, they accumulate possessions. And when that's your objective, you end up possessed by your possessions. You don't own them; they own you.

There is a world of difference between *making a living* and *making a life.* Life isn't measured in dollars; it's measured in moments you can't put a price tag on. It's so easy to become a creature of habit, isn't it? We go through the routine day after day. And before we know it, we're just going through the motions. Don't settle for the status quo. For that matter, don't settle down at all, ever!

One of my favorite "philosophers" is Jack Handey of *Saturday Night Live* fame. And one of my favorite "Deep Thoughts" by Handey is this one: "When you die, if you get a choice between going to regular heaven or pie heaven, choose pie heaven. It might be a trick, but if it's not, mmmmm-mmm, boy."[1]

I know that is somewhere on the spectrum between silly and sacrilegious, but I choose pie heaven. I'd rather aim high and miss it than aim low and hit it. Don't settle for good. Seek God. And when you do, don't be surprised when God does immeasurably more than all you can ask or imagine!

The day you stop dreaming is the day you start dying.

The day you start dreaming is the day you really start living.

Test Dummy

To one degree or another, we all suffer from something called hindsight bias. After an event has occurred, it's the tendency to see that event as having been predictable, even probable. It's hard for us to imagine any outcome other than the actual one. And nowhere is this truer than with well-rehearsed Bible stories we've heard a hundred times. Instead of shock and awe, we assume the outcome. So we take the miracles for granted.

We know that Benaiah chased, caught, and killed the lion. But if you didn't know the final outcome, who would you have placed bets on? This story could have ended very differently, very badly. But even if it had, what a way to go out! Am I right? I don't have a death wish, but there are worse ways to die. Like in your sleep. I want to go out chasing after a five-hundred-pound lion!

Let me add a little disclaimer here: I'm not advocating *dumb*!

Here's a good rule of thumb: If you're going to get out of a boat in the middle of the Sea of Galilee, you'd better make sure that Jesus said, "Come." But if Jesus says, "Come," you'd better not stay in the boat. The challenge, of course, is discerning when to do what. Either way, the key is discerning the voice of God. If He says, "Stay," then stay. If He says, "Come," then come.

How do you discern the voice of God? It starts with the Word of God. If you want to get a word *from* God, get into the Word of God. That's how you learn to discern the voice of God. After all, it's the Spirit of God who inspired the Word of God. And when the Spirit of God quickens the Word of God, it's like hearing the voice of God in Dolby surround sound.

There is a time and a place to err on the side of caution. But if you always err on that side, it probably says more about your personality than it does about prudence. There is also a time to throw caution to the wind. But in my experience the time to throw caution to the wind is *after* you have exercised some caution.

On February 4, 1912, a French tailor named Franz Reichelt climbed the stairs to the observation deck of the Eiffel Tower. He had designed a parachute suit that he had tested on jump dummies from the fifth floor of his apartment building. Despite the fact that many of those dummy drops were unsuccessful, Reichelt got permission from the Parisian Prefecture of Police to jump. It was quite the spectacle, drawing thousands of onlookers despite freezing temperatures. Concerned friends tried to convince Reichelt to experiment with dummies first, but he was absolutely convinced his jump suit would work. I admire his courage, but it was dumb not to use test dummies first. Reichelt's tragic fall left a 5.9-inch indentation in the frozen ground.[2]

Before you take a step of faith, get the facts. Dumb doesn't honor God. Due diligence does. Do your homework. As Paul said to his understudy Timothy, "Study to show yourself approved unto God."[3] This exhortation refers to the study of Scripture, but I think it's true of any subject matter.

Faith doesn't ignore facts, but it doesn't ignore God either. It confronts the brutal facts with unwavering faith.[4] It carefully counts the cost, and then it adds almighty God into the final equation.

No Fear

My grandma Alene Johnson was a short woman. If I remember right, I passed her in back-to-back measurements when I was in the fifth grade. She was five feet tall on tiptoes and quite frail. Toward the end of her eighty-four-year life, we would ask my good-natured grandma to show us her muscles. She'd attempt to flex, but instead of her bicep bulging, lots of loose skin would dangle beneath her arm. Then we'd jiggle it. I know that sounds unkind, but my fun-loving grandma would laugh every time.

My grandma was small in stature, but she was a spiritual giant. The story I'm about to share is legend in our family, but it's fact-check true. In her sixties my grandma ran her own floral business. She owned an oversized van to deliver flowers, but one day it was stolen. The police weren't making much progress in their investigation, so my grandma decided to play private investigator. She had a hunch that some kids had stolen it, so she patrolled the neighborhood around Columbia Heights High School just outside Minneapolis. Sure enough, she found her van parked outside the school. I'm not recommending this at all, but instead of calling the police, my grandma got inside the van and hid in the back. When the school bell rang, a couple of teenage boys got in, and my grandma scared the living daylights out of them. "Hello, boys," she said. "You stole my van!" Then my five-foot-nothing grandma marched them into the principal's office!

Go, Grandma!

Now here's the rest of the story.

My grandma grew up with a mother who was crippled by fear. Her father worked for the Sioux City and Pacific Railroad, so he was out of town quite a bit. And when he was, her mother had all the kids sleep in her room because she was deathly afraid. The last thing she did at night was push the dresser in front of the bedroom door! When my grandma grew up, she decided she'd never live that way, that she'd never be afraid of anything.

You can make the same decision.

Half of faith is learning what we don't know.

The other half is unlearning irrational fears and false assumptions.

Psychologists tell us that we're born with two fears—the fear of falling and the fear of loud noises. Every other fear is learned, which means that every other fear can be unlearned. Faith is the process of unlearning those fears. "Perfect love casts out fear."[5]

The opposite of love is not hate.

The opposite of love is fear.

True love leads to fearlessness.

The only difference between scaredy-cats and lion chasers is love. It's the love of God that sets us free from the spirit of fear. When you know that God loves you no matter what, you're not afraid to fail, because you know that God will be right there to pick you up if you fall down.

The cure for the fear of failure isn't success. The cure for the fear of failure is failure in small enough doses that we build up an immunity to it.

God is in the business of helping us overcome our fears, but He often does it by bringing us face to face with our worst fears. He graciously brings us back to the place of failure, and then He not only helps us pick up the broken pieces but He also puts them back together again.

Call Me Crazy

When a lion's roar registers in the auditory cortex, the brain sends an immediate message to the body: *run away as fast and as far as you can.* That's the normal reaction, but lion chasers aren't normal. They don't run away from what they're afraid of; they run toward the roar. They don't seek safety; they seek situations that scare them to life. Lion chasers are more afraid of missing opportunities than making mistakes.

He chased a lion.

We read right past it. So read it again.
That's the epitome of crazy!
One of my favorite catch phrases is "Call me crazy!" Not only do I consider it a supreme compliment, but I think it's one key to discerning the will of God. In my experience there is always an element of crazy in God's plans and purposes. Again, I'm not advocating dumb crazy, like the guys who take off their shirts in subfreezing temperatures at football games because they've had a few too many. I am, however, advocating an occasional decision that flies in the face of the facts, that spits in the face of the status quo.

David's mighty men were more than a little crazy; they were a lot crazy!

But they were simply reflecting what they saw in David. The epic example was his challenging Goliath to a fight, but that wasn't the only instance when David got his crazy on.

When he was in the custody of King Achish of Gath, the same Gath that Goliath came from, David was "very much afraid." He had killed Gath's favorite son, Goliath. And he expected the same treatment.

> So he pretended to be insane in their presence; and while he was in their hands he acted like a madman, making marks on the doors of the gate and letting saliva run down his beard.[6]

Letting saliva run down his beard? I'm picturing a crazed Jack Nicholson in *One Flew Over the Cuckoo's Nest* or any one of his psychopathic roles for that matter! David gave the performance of a lifetime, and it saved his life. The key? He got crazy! I'm not recommending this at special occasions like weddings, unless you are in fact the crazy uncle. But there are moments in life when you have to get outside your personality and get your crazy on.

Our move to Washington, DC, was a little crazy. We had no place to live and no guaranteed salary when we got here. Attempting a church plant in the nation's capital two years after failing in Chicago was crazy. And turning a crackhouse into a coffeehouse was a lot crazy.

Nathan Belete is an Ivy League–educated economist with the World Bank who served on our original leadership team at National Community Church. When we had the harebrained idea of turning that crackhouse into a coffeehouse, Nathan called it crazy. And Nathan was absolutely right. I'm not sure the idea would have passed muster at the World Bank, but Nathan didn't let crazy get in the way of what he believed was a God idea. If God was in it, he was for it. And that crazy idea turned out to be crazy awesome!

You can run away from what you're afraid of, but you'll be running the rest of your life. At some point you have to face your fear. And when you do, you'll discover that fear itself is a coward in the face of courage.

Go. Set. Ready.

One of my prized possessions is a lion spike. A lion spike is made of cow bone that has been sharpened on both ends and has a hand hole in the middle. It's the weapon of choice in the Maasai tribe when charging a lion. When the lion roars, the warrior thrusts the spike into its mouth. When the lion closes its jaws, the spike punctures the upper and lower jaws, making it impossible for the lion to bite down.

I don't know what dream you're chasing, what fear you're facing. But there is always a moment of truth when you have to dare to thrust the spike in the lion's mouth.

We have a mantra at NCC: "Go. Set. Ready." We inverted the old axiom "Ready, set, go," because if you wait until you're ready, you'll be waiting until the day you die!

I wasn't ready to get married. We weren't ready to have kids. I wasn't ready to plant a church. We weren't ready to go multisite. And I wasn't ready to write my first or second or thirteenth book.

You'll never be ready.

The issue isn't readiness; it's willingness.

We have a free-market system of small groups at National Community Church, which means we don't tell our leaders what to do. We let our leaders get a vision from God and go for it. That doesn't mean we never red-light an idea, but we've created a green-light culture. Why? Because two thousand years ago Jesus said, "Go."

Jesus also said, "I will build my church, and the gates of hell shall not prevail against it."[7] Gates are defensive measures. In other words, we're called to play offense. Faithfulness isn't holding down the fort until Jesus returns. Faithfulness is taking back enemy territory by shining light in dark places.

At the end of our lives, our greatest regrets won't be the mistakes we made. It'll be the opportunities we left on the table. Dr. Neal Roese calls them inaction regrets. And timing is a key factor. A study by social psychologists Tom Gilovich and Vicki Medvec found that in the short term, we tend to regret actions more than inactions 53 percent to 47 percent. So it's a tossup. But over the long haul, inaction regrets outnumber action regrets 84 percent to 16 percent.[8]

Our greatest regret at the end of our lives will be the lions we didn't chase.

Run to the roar!

SNOWY DAY

On a snowy day
2 Samuel 23:20

ON JULY 9, 1776, General George Washington was headquartered on Manhattan Island. The ink on the Declaration of Independence was less than a week old when Washington rallied his troops by having it read to them. Twenty-seven grievances were summarized in one revolutionary sentence: "A Prince whose character is thus marked by every act which may define a Tyrant, is unfit to be the ruler of a free people." That sentence lit a fuse.[1]

A few years earlier, in 1770, a fifteen-foot statue of King George III sitting on his high horse had been erected where Broadway dead-ends at Bowling Green. And that's where Washington's energized army marched right after the Declaration was read. They threw ropes around that two-ton lead statue and pulled it down. Then they put the broken pieces into wagons, took them down to the wharf, and placed them on a schooner that sailed up the East River to a foundry in Litchfield, Connecticut, where King George III was melted down and made into 42,088 musket balls.[2]

David's mighty men felt about King Saul the way Washington's army felt about King George III. Saul was a tyrant who had lost his conscience somewhere along the way. In my opinion he lost it the moment he set up a monument to himself at Mount Carmel.[3] When you stop building altars to God and start building monuments to yourself, it's the beginning of the end.

Pulling down the statue of King George III was an epic moment in the

American Revolution. It was the way Washington's troops declared their independence. It was the way they pledged their lives, fortunes, and sacred honor to the cause of freedom.

The symbolism is hard to miss, but I love the practicality too. The rebels didn't just pull it down; they melted it down. They turned that two-ton lead statue into 42,088 musket balls to shoot at King George III's redcoats. And I love the fact that someone took the effort to count them.

It's a beautiful picture of the way God works in our lives. God wants to redeem every attack the Enemy has waged against us. In fact, what the Enemy intends for evil, God will use for good.

Don't waste suffering.

Don't waste failure.

Don't waste disappointment.

Don't waste cancer.

Don't waste divorce.

God wants to recycle those things for His purposes!

Theory of Compensation

Around the turn of the twentieth century, Alfred Adler proposed the counterintuitive theory of compensation. Adler believed that perceived disadvantages often prove to be well-disguised advantages because they force us to develop attitudes and abilities that would have otherwise gone undiscovered. It's only as we compensate for those disadvantages that we discover our greatest gifts.[4]

Seventy percent of the art students Adler studied had optical anomalies. He observed that some of history's greatest composers, Mozart and Beethoven among them, had degenerative traces in their ears. And he cited a multiplicity of other examples, from a wide variety of vocations, of those who leveraged their weaknesses by discovering new strengths. Adler concluded that perceived disadvantages, such as birth defects, physical ailments, and poverty, can be springboards to success. And that success is not achieved *in spite* of those perceived disadvantages. It's achieved *because* of them.

Subsequent studies have added credibility to Adler's theory. In one study of small-business owners, for example, 35 percent were self-identified dyslexics.[5] While none of us would wish dyslexia on our children because of the academic challenge that comes with it, that disadvantage forced this group of entrepreneurs to cultivate different skill sets. Some of them became more proficient at oral communication because reading was so difficult. Others learned to rely on well-developed social skills to compensate for the challenges they faced in the classroom. And all of them cultivated a work ethic that might have remained dormant if reading had come easy for them.

Saul slept in the palace while David's band of brothers camped out in a cave. Saul's army was well equipped. David's mighty men were not, as evidenced by the fact that Benaiah had to snatch a spear out of the giant Egyptian's hand. And while Saul's army had food provided for them, David's men had to hunt and kill everything they ate.

Those disadvantages developed skills in David's mighty men that they didn't know they had. They had to work harder, grow stronger, and get smarter.

Destiny isn't revealed on sunny days. It's usually revealed on snowy days. Destiny isn't revealed while watching cute kitten videos. It's revealed when you cross paths with a five-hundred-pound lion. Destiny isn't just revealed in your natural gifts and abilities. It's also revealed in the compensatory skills you have to work extra hard to develop.

I felt called to preach when I was nineteen, but public speaking isn't a natural gifting for me. When I was in Bible college, I had friends who could preach a thirty-minute message from an outline on a three-by-five note card. Not me. Speaking extemporaneously didn't come naturally. I needed to study longer. Then I had to script and rescript every single word, every single time.

I thought my inability to speak extemporaneously was a preaching handicap, but it proved to be a writing advantage. Those sermon manuscripts, after some adaptations and alterations, would become book manuscripts. And without that perceived disadvantage, I doubt I would have cultivated my writing gifts. Writing, for me, is a compensatory skill.

You have gifts and abilities that you aren't even aware of, but they are often buried beneath perceived weaknesses. In those disadvantages, dreams are playing hide-and-seek.

No Excuse

It was the worst possible foe.

It was the worst possible place.

It was the worst possible conditions.

A snowy day isn't the best day to chase a sure-footed lion with claw cleats. As if the lion needed one more advantage, right? But what we perceive as negative circumstances are sometimes the best opportunities. Given the fact that lions can run thirty-six miles per hour, I'm pretty sure Benaiah couldn't keep up. But freshly fallen snow helped him track paw prints into the pit. Benaiah found a way to turn that disadvantage into an advantage.

When it comes to difficult circumstances, you have two choices. You can complain about them, or you can make the most of them. Whether those circumstances are self-inflicted or the result of someone else's actions, lion chasers make the most of them.

Sometimes the circumstances we're trying to change are the very circumstances God is using to change us. We ask God to change those circumstances, but God says, "No, I'm using those circumstances to change you!" Instead of expending all your energy trying to get out of them, get something out of them. In other words, learn the lesson God is trying to teach you.

"People are always blaming their circumstances for what they are," said George Bernard Shaw. "I don't believe in circumstances. The people who get on in this world are the people who get up and look for the circumstances they want, and if they can't find them, make them."[6]

Chasing a dream often starts with identifying and confessing your excuses. Here are some of the usual suspects: "I'm too young"; "I'm too old"; "I don't have enough education, enough experience, or enough money"; or

"I'm just not ready yet." Some excuses are more nuanced, like using your personality as a crutch.

When Sarah Careins was in high school, she dreamed of being a missionary, but she had a huge problem with shyness. "Then I realized that shyness was not my personality," she said. "My shyness was actually fear." Once Sarah called it what it was, the bondage of shyness was broken in her life. Sarah faced that fear, confessed the excuse, and now serves as a missionary in South Africa.

What excuse do you need to confess?

The Art of the Start

You cannot finish what you do not start.

In February of 2001, Thann Bennett felt called to write a book. "With some regularity," Thann said, "a fresh prompting would prick my conscience, and I would again consider toeing the starting line." But he would false start every single time.

Thann became an expert at excuses: *I don't have that kind of time. The book is outside the scope of my profession. These are the only years my wife and I have without children.*

"I was living in delayed obedience," admits Thann.

That all changed on April 19, 2015, when Thann heard a sermon I preached titled "The Art of the Start." Thann made a decision that day to give God one hour a day every day until the book he dreamed of writing was a reality.

It took Thann fifteen years to get to the starting line. It took him nine weeks to get to the finish line—a fifty-thousand-word manuscript.

What do you need to start?

First, give yourself a start date. And I'd highly recommend *today*! Second, give God an hour a day every day. It might mean getting up an hour earlier or staying up an hour later, but that's how dreams become reality. Third, give yourself a deadline. Deadlines are lifelines. Without them nothing gets done.

I leveraged my thirty-fifth birthday as a deadline for my first book, a self-published book titled *ID: The True You*. I gave myself forty days to write it, and I pulled it off.

How did I finish it? By starting it.

When I speak at writing conferences, I ask would-be authors one critical question: Are you called to write? If the answer is no, don't waste your time. If the answer is yes, then anything less is disobedience. Don't worry about getting an agent or finding a publisher.

Write for an audience of One.

Write as an act of obedience.

William Hutchison Murray said, "There is one elementary truth the ignorance of which kills countless ideas and splendid plans: that the moment one definitely commits oneself, the providence moves too. . . . Whatever you can do or dream you can, begin it. Boldness has genius, power, and magic in it."[7]

What do you need to start?

Maybe it's a diet. Maybe it's a graduate program. Maybe it's a church or a business. Whatever it is, you cannot finish what you do not start.

Begin it now!

Eighty Percent Certainty

One of the excuses I've confessed countless times is perfectionism. When coupled with procrastination, it's a dream killer. So when I meet a fellow perfectionist, I often prescribe the same passage of Scripture that cured my condition a decade ago. I prescribe Ecclesiastes 11:4 once a day for seven days, and it must be taken with meditation.

> Whoever watches the wind will not plant;
> whoever looks to the clouds will not reap.

If you're waiting for perfect conditions to pursue your dream, you'll be waiting till Christ returns. It doesn't matter whether a sunny day or a snowy day is forecast. At some point you need to throw caution to the wind. Do it after you've done your due diligence, but do it.

In 1998 I had a vision at the corner of Fifth and F Streets NE. I was walking down the street, as I had a thousand times before, when I had a vision of NCC meeting in movie theaters at metro stops all over the metro area. We now have eight campuses, but at the time *multisite* wasn't even a word.

We barely had one campus, so the thought of two campuses seemed overwhelming. Fast-forward five years, and I knew it was time to pull the trigger. I was dragging my feet until I encountered a paradigm shift on page 93 of Andy Stanley's book *The Next Generation Leader.*

> Generally speaking, you are probably never going to be more than about 80 percent certain. Waiting for greater certainty may cause you to miss an opportunity. Depending upon your personality, no amount of information may move you past a particular degree of certainty.[8]

Then Andy himself said, "I rarely get past about 80 percent."

That has been a rule of thumb for me ever since, except when it comes to marriage. Then I'd shoot for a little more than 80 percent certainty!

A few years later I was at a gathering of multisite churches listening to a former executive of Pepsi speaking. One sentence solidified the 80 percent rule: "I'd rather have an 80 percent plan 100 percent executed than a 100 percent plan 80 percent executed."

Don't let 80 percent certainty hold you back. Benaiah's odds were way less than that. Once you get a green light from God, it's go time. Then you have to find ways to make progress on your dream every day.

Go Time

A goal is a dream with a deadline.

No matter what dream God has given you, you have to break it down into manageable steps. You have to turn it into a to-do list, or it will never amount to more than a wish list. Give yourself a timeline and a deadline. That's what I did when I wrote my first self-published book a decade ago. I vowed to myself that I wouldn't turn thirty-five without a book to show for it. I gave myself forty days to write it. And I somehow pulled it off.

This may sound like a Jedi mind trick, but let me share one last idea that has helped tip the balance for me. Because of my perfectionism, I can spend an hour searching the thesaurus for the perfect word or half a day perfecting one paragraph. The problem with that approach is that it takes about ten years to write one book. So I've come to an agreement with my editors that once a chapter hits the 80 percent mark, I hit Send. Otherwise I'll work it and rework it ad infinitum.

It may sound as if I'm lowering my standard by settling for 80 percent, but I'm really not. When you're a perfectionist, the hardest part is tying off the umbilical cord on the first draft. The 80 percent rule relieves the pressure I put on myself, so I actually finish my first draft much faster. That saved time gives me two more cracks at a manuscript—line edits and final edits. Mathematically, that 80 percent approach, times three, gets me just shy of 100 percent.

Let me explain.

The first draft gets me to 80 percent certainty, 80 percent satisfaction. The second draft allows me to edit the 20 percent I'm not so sure of. Taking the same 80 percent approach with that 20 percent nets a 16 percent improvement. So now I'm at 96 percent perfection. And the third time is the charm! I take the same 80 percent approach with the final 4 percent, and that gets me to 99.2 percent. Then I round it up and call it a final manuscript!

No matter what dream you have, that 80 percent approach might help you overcome procrastination and perfectionism.

Henry James once wrote a story titled "The Madonna of the Future." It's a fictional account of an artist who devoted her entire life to a single painting. When the artist died, it was discovered that the canvas was blank.

She never finished because she never started, and she never started because of perfectionism.

That fictional story is nonfiction for far too many.

The nineteenth-century historian Lord Acton borrowed James's phrase to describe his own life's work about the history of liberty. It has been described as the greatest book never written. "Always discouraged by the imperfection of the material," said Daniel Boorstin, "he always delayed his unifying work by the promise of new facts and new ideas."[9]

What's your *Madonna of the Future*?

In first-century Israel there was a saying: "It's still four months until harvest."[10] Jesus rebuked it. "I tell you, open your eyes and look at the fields! They are ripe for harvest."[11]

Don't put off till tomorrow what God has called you to do today.

Delayed obedience is disobedience.

Seize the day![12]

Opportunity Cost

Remember Blockbuster? I sometimes miss those pilgrimages to pick out a movie. Of course, I don't miss getting home and realizing the wrong DVD was in the case. At their peak in 2004, Blockbuster had sixty thousand employees, nine thousand stores worldwide, and annual revenues of $5.9 billion.[13]

At the time only 4 percent of homes in America had a broadband connection. Key fact. But that number skyrocketed to 68 percent in 2010. In other words, the game changed, and the name of the game was video streaming.

Blockbuster ultimately filed for bankruptcy, but it didn't have to end that way. If only they hadn't turned down the opportunity to buy a DVD-mailing company called Netflix for $50 million in 2000. That might seem like a steep price tag, but it represented three days of Blockbuster revenues. Netflix's value now stands at $32.9 billion, exceeding the value of CBS![14]

Blockbuster missed an opportunity, and they have plenty of company. Yahoo turned down the opportunity to acquire Google, and Friendster turned down the opportunity to buy out Facebook.

In business speak, it's called an *opportunity cost.*

It's the loss of potential gain when an opportunity isn't seen and seized. But it's not just a forfeiture of possibilities; the collateral damage can be devastating. Counting the cost is a biblical principle, but it doesn't mean just the *actual cost.* That's the easy part. The hard part is calculating the *opportunity cost.*

In 2008 four students set out to revolutionize the eyewear industry by offering fashionable frames at a fraction of the price, *online.* Adam Grant was offered an opportunity to invest in Warby Parker, but he turned it down. Why? If it was a good idea, it would have already been done! Plus, who is going to buy prescription glasses online? The founders expected to sell a pair or two of glasses per day out of the gate, but they had to put twenty thousand orders on a waiting list their first month. In five years' time Warby Parker would be valued at more than $1 billion.[15]

Adam Grant said, "It was the worst financial decision I've ever made."[16]

It didn't cost him one penny in *actual cost.*

It did cost him millions in *opportunity cost.*

The key to success in business and success in life is an eye for opportunity. And despite the old aphorism, opportunity rarely knocks. You have to knock on it. And you'll probably have to knock more than once or twice.

Generally speaking, we see only what we're looking for. If you're looking for excuses, you will always find one. But the same is true for opportunities. If you look for them, you'll find them all around you all the time—even on a snowy day!

FIVE-POUND DREAM

He snatched the spear.

2 Samuel 23:21

SANTIAGO MONCADA REMEMBERS army-crawling through his house with bullets flying through the window when he was a little boy. He also remembers tanks driving down the street, helicopters hovering overhead, and bombs blowing up all around him. Santi's father worked as a chef for the guerillas who supplied cocaine to the Colombian cartel. In fact, he once threw a party for Pablo Escobar, the "King of Cocaine." At the height of his criminal career, Escobar was worth an estimated $100 billion as a result of supplying 80 percent of the cocaine smuggled into America.

Santi escaped the crime and violence with his mother and immigrated to America. But he left part of his heart in his native Colombia. In December of 2012 Santi made a pilgrimage back to his hometown of Miranda, nestled in the Cauca valley at the foothills of the Andes mountain range. Over breakfast with a local pastor, he was introduced to two farmers who had risked their lives and livelihoods to stop growing the coca plants that would ultimately turn into cocaine. They dreamed of becoming coffee farmers, but they didn't know how to export the dream God had given them. For three years they had prayed that God would show them how to fulfill their dream. That's when Santi showed up, and their dream became his dream.

Santi returned to America with five pounds of coffee beans and a dream called Redeeming Grounds. Last year they helped Colombian farmers in a conflict zone transition fifty-four acres from coca to coffee cultivation. In doing so, they took 1,740 kilos of coca paste out of production, with a street value of more than $85 million. What started out as a five-pound dream has turned into a five-hundred-pound lion as thousands of pounds of coffee are imported from converted coca farmers.

Redeeming Grounds is living up to, living out its name. It's not dissimilar to the dream God gave us for Ebenezers coffeehouse on Capitol Hill. A decade ago we turned a crackhouse into a coffeehouse. Our dream was coffee with a cause, giving every penny of profit to kingdom causes. What we didn't know was that our dream would help fulfill the dream of coffee farmers in Colombia via Santiago Moncada. Redeeming Grounds isn't just one of our roasters; they're the middleman between our dream and the dream of courageous coffee farmers in Colombia. The faces of those farmers whom Santi first met over breakfast now grace every bag of Redeeming Grounds coffee sold at Ebenezers coffeehouse.[1]

Whether you're aware of it or not, your dream is contingent upon someone else having the courage to pursue his or her dream. And someone else's dream is contingent upon you pursuing yours! Those Colombian farmers needed Santi, and Santi needed them.

We live in a culture of individualism that celebrates lone rangers, but even the Lone Ranger had Tonto. Without his mighty men David would have lived out his days as a political fugitive. And just as David needed them, they needed a dreamer like David to rally around. Our dreams are more interconnected with one another than any of us could ever imagine, and the best way to fulfill your dream is to help others fulfill theirs.

Dream Jealousy

Sometimes a picture is worth a thousand words.

Sometimes it's worth $27,000.

Santi recently sent me a fifteen-second selfie where he's holding a kilo of cocaine in his hand with a bonfire behind him. I don't know if Santi was scared, but I was scared for him! That kilo of coke has a street value of $27,000 once it crosses the border and gets into the wrong hands. The look on Santi's face as he tossed it into the fire had to be the same look Benaiah had on his face when he snatched the spear out of the hands of that giant Egyptian.

The key word is *snatched*. Benaiah did a little jujitsu—he used the Egyptian's weapon against him. Santi has perfected the same maneuver.

Every time I worship I try to key off a line of lyrics. It keeps my worship from becoming lip service. I often write the lyrics in my journal so I can meditate on them and pray into them. Then I put the song on repeat to let it get into my spirit. A recent favorite is "Sovereign over Us" by Aaron Keyes. Part of the reason I like it is that I like Aaron. And his lyrics are a great paraphrase of Genesis 50:20: *what the Enemy means for evil, God uses for our good and for His glory.*

Remember the story of Joseph? His heartless brothers faked his death and sold him to human traffickers. Then things went from bad to worse, and Joseph ended up in an Egyptian dungeon. Thirteen years later, in the most amazing rise to political power ever, Joseph became Pharaoh's right-hand man. That's when his brothers came begging for food. But instead of taking revenge on his brothers, Joseph said, "You intended to harm me, but God intended it for good to accomplish what is now being done, the saving of many lives."[2]

Let me reverse-engineer this.

Do you remember why his brothers sold him into slavery in the first place? The short answer is Genesis 37:8: "They hated him all the more because of his dream." They mockingly called Joseph "that dreamer."[3]

Your dreams will inspire many people, no doubt. But your dreams will also summon opposition. Why? Because you are disrupting the status quo. Your dreams will cause a wide variety of reactions, including jealousy and anger. Some people might even want to kill you because of them. Santi can testify to that.

Every time Santi helps convert a cocoa field into a coffee farm, he's snatching the spear out of the drug dealers' hands. Like Benaiah, he's putting his life at risk. But when you experience that kind of opposition, see it as affirmation! The Enemy wouldn't mess with you if you weren't messing with him. Opposition from the Enemy is often a good sign, a vital sign. You're on the verge of a breakthrough.

Every dreamer has to deal with naysayers, and I've had more than my fair share. So let me share how I've dealt with criticism. First, don't let an arrow of criticism pierce your heart unless it first passes through the filter of Scripture.[4] Second, you have to come to terms with the fact that you can please all of the people some of the time and some of the people all of the time, but you cannot please all of the people all of the time. You're going to offend someone, so you have to decide who. My advice? Offend Pharisees! Jesus did it with intentionality and regularity. Your dream is going to ruffle some feathers, but don't play chicken. Operate in a spirit of bold humility knowing that God goes before you. And remember this: a compliment from a fool is really an insult, and an insult from a fool is really a compliment. Make sure you consider the source.

Measured in Dollars

Throwing a kilo of cocaine into a bonfire reminds me of the bonfire in Acts 19:19. They weren't toasting marshmallows either!

> A number who had practiced sorcery brought their scrolls together and burned them publicly. When they calculated the value of the scrolls, the total came to fifty thousand drachmas.

A drachma was a silver coin worth a day's wages. Based on the median income in DC, they burned $12,328,767 worth of scrolls in today's dollars. That is a statement of faith, a financial statement. We don't typically measure dreams in dollars, but in my opinion it took $27,000 worth of faith for Santi to throw that kilo of coke into the fire.

Sometimes faith can be measured in dollars.

There comes a moment in every dream journey when you have to put your money where your dream is. It might be a $50 date, a $100 application fee, a $500 plane ticket, or a $2,000 lease. Think of it as a down payment on your dream.

At different points in my dream journey, I've taken $50 steps of faith, $85 steps of faith, $400 steps of faith, $5,000 steps of faith, and a few much larger steps of faith. When we purchased the crackhouse on Capitol Hill, it required $325,000 worth of faith, plus the legal fees to get it rezoned as a commercial property. Then it took $2.7 million worth of faith to build it.

Whether it's a for-profit or nonprofit dream, it takes dollars to fund it. If you have the cash up front, count your blessings. If you don't, you might need to get creative with crowd funding. But don't feel as if you're at a disadvantage if you don't have an angel investor. The more money you have to raise, the more faith you'll develop early in your dream journey.

Our budget at National Community Church is now eight digits, but I remember when our gross income was $2,000 a month. We weren't even self-supporting until our third year. It was stressful at the time, but those lean years kept us grounded and grateful. And we're better stewards of the millions God has entrusted to us now simply because we had to pinch pennies then. In fact, we still pinch pennies.

Dream Markers

In every dream journey there is a point of no return. It's a decision that cannot be undone, like chasing a lion into a pit or throwing a kilo of coke into the fire. Sometimes it's a rule you break, a risk you take, or a sacrifice you make. And once you break it, take it, or make it, there is no turning back. I call them dream markers. And Scripture is full of them.

In the Old Testament it's Abraham putting Isaac on the altar. It's Moses saying to Pharaoh, "Let my people go." It's Rahab harboring Jewish spies. It's David taking off Saul's armor. It's Esther entering the king's court uninvited.

In the New Testament it's the wise men following the star. It's Andrew dropping his fishing nets. It's Zacchaeus climbing the sycamore tree. It's

Peter getting out of the boat. It's Jesus surrendering Himself to God in the Garden of Gethsemane and then surrendering to the religious mob.

In the plot line of our lives, dream markers are defining decisions. They aren't just part of the narrative; they become metanarratives. As far as we know, Benaiah chased only one lion. Granted, that's one more than anybody I know! But it was more than just a one-off. It became a storyline, as evidenced by the adverb used to describe the two Moabites he slew: *lionlike*.[5]

One moment defined his life—in a pit with a lion on a snowy day.

One decision defined his approach to life—chase the lion.

A few years ago I spent a few days with a life coach putting together a life plan. In one of the exercises, I identified thirty-nine turning points. Each of them changed the trajectory of my life, but a few rank as dream markers. One such marker was giving up a full-ride scholarship at the University of Chicago and transferring to Central Bible College.

When I walked into the admissions office at the University of Chicago to notify them of my desire to transfer, I knew it was a decision that could not be undone. I not only gave up a full-ride scholarship at the U of C, but I also had to pay out of pocket for my education at CBC. On paper it was a net loss of $92,500 over two and a half years. I didn't think about it in these terms then, but the decision to transfer took $92,500 worth of faith. Of course, the net gain is impossible to quantify.

Every dream has a price tag. There is dream tax too, and don't forget about all the hidden costs! But a God-sized dream is worth every penny, every second, every ounce of energy.

How much is your dream worth?

Pay the Price

One of the defining moments in our dream journey as a church was the decision to start giving to missions *before* we were self-supporting. It was a financial statement of faith based on a core conviction: God will bless us in proportion to how we give to missions. In the last decade NCC has given

$8,957,527 to missions. This past year we hit a new high—$2,005,000. But it started with $50 faith.

Twenty years ago when I first felt impressed to start giving to missions, I was reticent. How can you give what you don't have? I felt that God needed to tap someone else to give to us, not the other way around. Plus, what difference could $50 make? Well, we quickly discovered that it makes a 200 percent difference in God's economy! Our giving tripled the next month, and we've never looked back.

Nothing sets us up for God's provision like sacrificial giving. If you want God to bless you beyond your ability, try giving beyond your means. Now, a material reward isn't what we're after. That's the least reward. We're after an eternal reward in heaven. But one way or the other, this promise holds true: "Give, and it will be given to you. A good measure, pressed down, shaken together and running over, will be poured into your lap. For with the measure you use, it will be measured to you."[6]

You cannot break the law of measures. It will make or break you. The bigger your dream, the greater investment of time, talent, and treasure it will take to accomplish it. God-sized dreams require more risk, more sacrifice, and more faith.

One of the dream markers in our dream journey of building a coffee-house was an auction where I bid $85 on a two-inch-thick zoning guide-book published by the Capitol Hill Restoration Society. We didn't own 201 F Street NE yet. But if by some miracle we were able to purchase it, I knew we'd need to get it rezoned. That guidebook, filled with rules and regulations, had to be the least sexy item up for bid. And if we didn't get a contract on that property, it was a waste of money, a waste of paper. But the dream was worth an $85 bid.

How much is your dream worth?

Is it worth $50? How about $85?

What price are you willing to pay?

The law of measures is more than a financial principle. It applies to every facet of life. The nicer you are to others, the nicer others will be to you.

In other words, what goes around comes around. But money is most often where the rubber meets the road. When God gives a vision, He makes provision. But in my experience, you often have to take a financial step of faith first.

So one last time: How much is your dream worth?

Count the cost.

Pay the price.

Repeat as necessary!

DOUBLE DESTINY

He too was as famous as the three mighty warriors.

2 Samuel 23:22

IN AUGUST OF 1989 God awakened me in the middle of the night, led me to the first chapter of Jeremiah, and revealed my calling with one verse of Scripture. Nothing like it had ever happened before, and nothing like it has happened since. It was a one-off. For what it's worth, it happened one week after my prayer walk through the cow pasture where I felt called to ministry. God knew that I might need two signs—just as Gideon did.

I knelt at the foot of my bed, opened my Bible, and started reading.

Before I formed you in the womb I knew you,
    before you were born I set you apart;
    I appointed you as a prophet to the nations.[1]

No passage of Scripture is more personal to me than this one. It's my matrix for ministry. I own it and it owns me. It's not just Jeremiah's calling; I feel as though it's my calling. But there's a catch. One caveat of that calling made no sense to me: "I appointed you as a prophet to the nations."

Honestly, I didn't feel called to the nations; I felt called to our nation's capital. I didn't feel called to be a missionary; I felt called to be a pastor. This verse of Scripture, this part of my script, wouldn't make sense for more than two decades. That's when I got an e-mail from a pastor friend named Bryan Jarrett. And the veil that had covered my eyes was lifted.

I'm speaking at a leadership conference for the nation of Malaysia and visited the largest bookstore in Kuala Lumpur today. I was thrilled to see a copy of your book *Soulprint* in a very visible place. I stopped to praise God for the influence He has given you to the nations!

I had never before connected the dots between my calling to write and God's desire to use me to speak to the nations. It had never even crossed my mind that my books would be translated into dozens of different languages. I don't speak a lick of Korean or Russian or Afrikaans or Kinyarwanda. I speak English and just enough Spanish to order chili con queso. Pretty sad for four years of study! But through the work of interpreters, my books have been used to convey God's grace, truth, and love all around the world.

Just as my writing has fulfilled this calling without my even knowing it, so has pastoring a church in Washington, DC. Twenty years in, the sun never sets on our missionary family all around the globe. And our podcast reaches 144 countries, some of which are closed to Christianity.

But I hadn't really thought of NCC as a prophet to the nations until Dick Foth called me on a recent Sunday afternoon. Dick had just spoken at one of our campuses and wanted to tell me whom he had met—a family that had emigrated from China, a woman from Mongolia who had won a green card and moved to America, and the German wife of an American who had just been appointed consul general in Hamburg, Germany. Believe it or not, that is pretty par for the course at NCC. I had actually met a member of Finland's parliament that same day at a different campus. But I had never really connected the dots until Dick emphatically said, "Mark, stay right where you are! You can reach the nations!"

That's when it dawned on me, once again, that God has been fulfilling His calling without my even knowing it. God has strategically positioned NCC for such a place as this. We're not only reaching members of the military, State Department emissaries, and international businesspeople, but we're sending them to the four corners of the globe as ambassadors for Christ.

When David took harp lessons as a kid, he never imagined that those lessons would someday position him as a member of King Saul's court. As he practiced slinging a stone while tending sheep, it never crossed his mind that this skill set would catapult him into the national limelight. Even when David was hiding out in caves as a fugitive, God was deepening his emotional capacity to write psalms that would pull heartstrings thousands of years later.

Just because something isn't part of your life plan doesn't mean it's not part of God's plan. God is working His good, pleasing, and perfect plan for your life in a thousand ways you aren't even aware of. Everything in your past is preparation for something in your future. God wastes nothing! Even when you have a setback, God has already prepared your comeback. The God who works all things together for good will leverage every experience, every skill, every mistake, and every bit of knowledge you have acquired.

Predestined

Whenever Scripture doubles down on a truth by saying the same thing in two different ways, it deserves a double take. It's God's way of making doubly sure we don't miss the point. For example, "With God all things are possible."[2] And just to make sure we're picking up what He is throwing down, Scripture says, "Nothing will be impossible with God."[3]

The same concept is repeated twice in Jeremiah 1:5: "before I formed you in the womb" and "before you were born." Your destiny predates you. Before you were even conceived, God had a script for your life.

The irony of destiny is that it's rarely discerned at the time. Sometimes it's not revealed until after we die. David reigned over a kingdom of millions, but his psalms have inspired billions. That is David's longest legacy, whether he knew it at the time or not. And I'm guessing not. Your greatest influence might be posthumous. It's one more way God gets the last laugh and the glory!

When we zoom out and look through a wide-angle lens, I think it's fair to say that our Founding Fathers have had more influence in death than in life. And that's true of spiritual fathers as well. Your greatest legacy might be the children or church or charitable trusts that outlive you. For the record, this is one reason I write. Books are time capsules. I write because I want my great-great-grandchildren to know what I lived for and what I was willing to die for. And if others want to read my books while I'm living, all the better. But I write for the third and fourth generation.

"Before I formed you in the womb." This phrase should fill you with a sense of destiny. It's your spiritual birthright. God has ordained your days, ordered your footsteps, and prepared good works in advance. And He did it before you were even conceived.

One reason I love this seven-word phrase so much is that it reminds me of my firstborn son, Parker. Two decades ago I was preaching at a church in DC, pre-NCC. After I finished preaching, the pastor prayed for Lora and me. At some point that prayer became prophetic. Pastor Sullivan McGraw turned toward Lora and prayed, "Lord, bless the little one that is within." That was news to us! But sure enough, the doctor confirmed it the next week. We're the only couple I've ever heard of who found out they were pregnant during a prayer at church!

Posthumous

For the past decade I've served as a trustee for the Des Plaines Charitable Trust. It's not a large foundation, but it has given millions of dollars to kingdom causes over the past quarter century.

In 1985 a businessman on the verge of bankruptcy walked into a prayer meeting. Jim Linen was desperate, so desperate that he struck a deal with God. He put his business, the Des Plaines Publishing Company, on the altar. He knew it'd take a miracle to dodge bankruptcy, so Jim made a pledge. If God would bless his business, he'd create a trust fund that would fund kingdom causes.

On July 2, 1989, Jim was tragically killed while jogging in London. His life on earth came to an end, but Jim's legacy had just begun. At the annual meeting of the trust, we often read the original trust document that Jim drafted:

This trust is created in fulfillment of a pledge James A. Linen IV made to the Lord when Des Plaines Publishing Company was, by every known business standard, a bankrupt entity, as, in truth, was he. Following Mr. Linen's commitment, the success of Des Plaines in the face of both national and local economic conditions can only be viewed as a miracle of God.

Destiny predates birth.
Destiny postdates death.
The trust has given grants to a thousand kingdom causes around the globe, and each one is an exponential of Jim Linen's legacy. It could be argued that Jim's influence is greater in death than it was in life. And when we follow in Christ's footsteps, the same is true of us.

As Famous As

If your goal is fame, good luck. Even if you achieve it, you'll realize that it's as unfulfilling as fortune. You don't need a bigger paycheck. You need a bigger *why*. Our chief end is to glorify God, and if your goal is to make famous the name of Jesus, good fortune will follow you all the days of your life and right into eternity!

He too was as famous as the three mighty warriors.[4]

That little three-word phrase, "as famous as," is repeated several times in 2 Samuel 23. It refers to Benaiah, but fame wasn't his objective. In fact, his destiny was to help David fulfill his dream. It wasn't about Benaiah. It was about David.

In her spirit Julie Neal felt as if she was on the verge of something big. In fact, God told her to *get ready*! She just wasn't sure how or for what. That's when she visited her brother and sister-in-law, who had adopted a baby from Africa. On the way home Julie's eight-year-old daughter said, "We need to adopt a baby." Julie quickly came up with all kinds of excuses, but she had run out of excuses by the time she pulled into her driveway. She knew in her spirit this was exactly what God had been getting her ready for.

A year later the Neal family adopted Caden from Ethiopia. Two years later they adopted Cruz. Then in 2010 Julie visited the village in Ethiopia where Cruz had been born. It's the place where her son took his first breath and his biological mother took her last breath. When Julie asked Cruz's grandparents how his mother died, they said she died because they didn't have anywhere to take her to get medical treatment. That's the day a dream was conceived in Julie's spirit. Her first step was raising $200,000 to build a well in memory of Cruz's mom. Cruz actually dedicated that well, a posthumous gift in memory of his mother. They built a school a year later. And Julie won't stop dreaming until a medical center is built.

"If God had laid the entire dream out in front of me at the beginning of this journey, I would have run away from it," said Julie.

In His grace God doesn't always download the entire dream at one time. It would overwhelm us. But make no mistake: His plans and purposes are beyond what you can ask. And He wants to use you in ways you cannot imagine.

Your job isn't to accomplish the dream.

Your job is to stop making excuses and start obeying.

"God gives us a little piece of the plan at a time," Julie said. "And if we keep focusing on Him, it all falls into place—sometimes slowly and painfully. But it all falls into place."

One fun footnote. The organization that Julie serves, I Pour Life, is one of the kingdom causes that Des Plaines has funded.[5] Des Plaines is a very small piece of the puzzle, but I Pour Life is still part of Jim Linen's legacy—a dream within a dream.

Double Destiny

You have a destiny, but you don't just have one. You have two—one is universal, and the other is unique. Think of it as your double destiny.

Just as we share a common grace, we all share a common destiny. We are predestined to be conformed to the image of Christ.[6] In other words, our universal destiny is to think like, act like, love like, and be like the prototype—Jesus. If you pursue that common destiny, it will lead to an uncommon life. You'll go places you can't get to. You'll do things beyond your capabilities. And you'll meet people you have no business being in the same room with. But the goal isn't going, doing, or meeting. The ultimate goal is becoming like Christ.

We all share that destiny in common, but the other destiny is unique.

There never has been and never will be anyone like you. Of course, that isn't a testimony to you. It's a testimony to the God who created you. And it means that no one can worship God like you or for you. If uniqueness is God's gift to you, then individuation is your gift back to God. We all need heroes who inspire us, but you aren't called to be more like them. You are called to be you—the best version of you possible.

Like happiness, destiny isn't something you discover by seeking it. It's a by-product. You don't find it by looking for it. You find it by looking for God. Then your destiny finds you.

Hold that thought.

Mel Gibson lionized Sir William Wallace in his epic film *Braveheart*. It's tough to discern fact from fiction when it comes to medieval knights, but one biographer noted that Wallace actually killed a lion during a trip to France.[7] One fact is certain, however: Wallace never went anywhere without his Psalter. As a fugitive and as a warrior, Wallace identified with the psalms of David in a unique way. And just as David had Benaiah always at his side, Wallace never went anywhere without his boyhood friend and personal chaplain, John Blair.[8]

I'm reading between the lines, but Benaiah was more than a bodyguard. He didn't just protect David's back; he also had David's ear. Benaiah was to King David what John Blair was to Sir William Wallace. Benaiah was David's closest confidant, a kindred spirit. He was more of a brother than some of David's brothers. Perhaps that's why David's son Solomon trusted him like an uncle.

I have a friend, Joshua DuBois, who chased a lion into the White

House. Joshua served as the head of the Office of Faith-Based and Neighborhood Partnerships. "I went to policy school, not seminary," he noted. But Joshua understood that even if you report to the president, you still answer to a higher authority. For seven years Joshua was a priest to POTUS, sharing a word of encouragement from Scripture every single day.⁹ His unique destiny was serving the president of the United States; of course, his higher calling was serving God.

No matter what you do, you are a priest first and foremost. You certainly have a job to do, but you also have a calling to fulfill. If you are a Christ follower, you are part of the royal priesthood. That means you are a priest-entrepreneur, priest-athlete, priest-entertainer, priest-politician, priest-coach.

Your portfolio is your pulpit.

Your company is your congregation.

And that goes for your team, your class, or your organization.

Destiny isn't pie in the sky. Destiny is being faithful right where you are. The best way to land your dream job is to do a good job at a bad job and do it with a great attitude!

Be like Christ.

Be yourself.

That's your double destiny.

CHAIN REACTION

And David put him in charge of his bodyguard.

2 Samuel 23:23

IN 1983 LORNE WHITEHEAD published an article in the *American Journal of Physics* about the domino chain reaction.[1] You can picture it in your mind, can't you? You knock over a domino, and it sets off a chain reaction that can knock down hundreds of dominoes in a matter of seconds. But the unique significance of Whitehead's research was discovering that a domino is capable of knocking over a domino that is one-and-a-half times its size. So a two-inch domino can topple a three-inch domino. A three-inch domino can topple a four-and-a-half-inch domino. And a four-and-a-half-inch domino can topple . . . Well, you get the point.

By the time you get to the eighteenth domino, you could knock over the Leaning Tower of Pisa. Of course, it's leaning so that's not fair. The twenty-third domino could knock over the Eiffel Tower. And by the time you get to the twenty-eighth domino, you could take down the Empire State Building.

In the realm of mathematics, there are two types of progression: linear and exponential. Linear progression is two plus two equals four. Exponential progression is compound doubling. Four times four equals sixteen. If you take thirty linear steps, you're ninety feet from where you started. But if you take thirty exponential steps, you've circled the earth twenty-six times![2]

Faith isn't linear.

Faith is exponential.

Every decision we make, every risk we take, has a chain reaction. And those chain reactions set off a thousand chain reactions we aren't even aware of. The cumulative effect won't be revealed until we reach the other side of the space-time continuum.

It takes very little effort to push over a tiny domino, only .024 joules of input energy. You can do it with your pinky finger. By the time you reach the thirteenth domino, the gravitational potential energy is two billion times greater than the energy it took to knock over that first domino.[3] My point? Some of us want to start with the Leaning Tower of Pisa or the Eiffel Tower or the Empire State Building. Good luck with that.

Benaiah didn't start out chasing five-hundred-pound lions; he probably started out chasing a cute little kitten named Killer. He didn't start out with two lionlike Moabites; he started out in the seventy-eight-pound weight class in middle school.

Don't despise the day of small beginnings!

Your two-inch domino might seem insignificant, but extrapolated across space and time, it can make all the difference in the world. If you do little things like they're big things, God will do big things like they're little things.

All Aboard

On May 17, 1902, Christian Schmidgall boarded a ship in Antwerp, Belgium, and set sail for America. According to the ship's manifest, he was sixteen years old, had ten dollars to his name, and didn't speak a lick of English.

After landing on Ellis Island, Christian boarded a train bound for central Illinois, where he took odd jobs to make ends meet. After renting a farm for many years, he saved enough money to buy eighty acres of farmland in Minier, Illinois. That farm is still in our family. Christian planted oats and hay; his great-great-grandson produces beans and corn. But the seeds Christian planted are reaping a harvest to the third and fourth generations.

The domino effect of that one decision is mind boggling. If Christian

Schmidgall had stayed in the tiny village of Walkensweiler, Germany, I doubt I would have met and married his great-granddaughter. But because he pursued his dream, I met my dream girl.

I'm not convinced that Christian Schmidgall was thinking of the third generation when he immigrated to America. He was only a teenager, after all. Plus, we tend to think of our decisions in present-tense terms. We think right here, right now. But God is the God of three generations—the God of Abraham, the God of Isaac, the God of Jacob.

Forty years after immigrating, Christian Schmidgall put his faith in Jesus Christ. God became the God of Christian, and He eventually became the God of Edgar, the God of Bob, and the God of his great-granddaughter and my wife, Lora.

Every decision we make has a domino effect way beyond our ability to predict or control. We can't predict when or where or how, but our seeds of faith will reap a harvest somehow, someway, someday. And it's often when and where we least expect it.

Benaiah didn't know he was updating and upgrading his LinkedIn profile when he took down two of Moab's mightiest warriors. He didn't know that chasing a lion into a pit on a snowy day was a networking event, earning him entrée to David's inner circle. That wasn't his motivation, but it was God's ulterior motive. Whether you know it or not, God is building your résumé.

Can't you picture David flipping through résumés?

Law enforcement major, University of Jerusalem.

Internship, palace guard.

Driver, Brinks Armored Chariots.

David yawns.

Killed a lion in a pit on a snowy day.

Winner, winner, chicken dinner! When can you start? I bet David didn't even check references.

So David hired Benaiah, but he wasn't just employing a bodyguard. Without even knowing it, David was grooming his son's commander in chief.

Far Off

We think that what God does for us is for us, but it's never just for us. It's always for the third and fourth generations. We think right here, right now, but God is thinking nations and generations.

Matt Geppert is a lion chaser, the son of lion chasers. Matt recently assumed leadership of SEAPC, the South East Asia Prayer Center, which his parents founded in 1991. Eight years ago we made a financial investment in SEAPC, but I hadn't given it much thought until Matt e-mailed me an update.

> The work NCC supported eight years ago, when I first wrote to you about Tibet and Cambodia, has exploded. Today, we are the first international organization to be certified by the government of China to train trainers in autism, reaching 15 million homes with a government certified spiritual approach to an unanswered disease. This spring we have expanded from 8 to 488 public schools, from 8,000 to 126,000 students who are learning a Christ-based curriculum in the province of Banteay Meanchey.

You have no idea where Banteay Meanchey even is, do you? And neither do I. But we planted a seed eight years ago that is bearing fruit in a remote province halfway around the world.

> The promise is for you and your children and for all who are far off.[4]

What's true of the promise in Acts 2:39 is true of every promise in Scripture. There is no statute of limitations—chronological or geographical. The promise is for you, but it's not *just* for you. It's for the second generation—"your children." It's for nations and generations—"all who are far off."

Chronologically, we're two thousand years removed from the Day of Pentecost. But there is no expiration date on God's promises. Geographically, Washington, DC, is 5,914 miles from the place where the apostle Peter proclaimed this promise. That's far off, but it's not beyond the reach of God's providence.

Second-Generation Influence

Thirty years ago my father-in-law officiated at the wedding of Kent and Karen Ingle. Karen's father, Glenn Kraiss, was a longstanding board member at Calvary Church, the church where my father-in-law served as pastor. Three decades later I have the joy and privilege of serving on the board of Southeastern University, where Kent serves as president. My daughter, Summer, is a student at SEU. The seeds that Summer's grandfather sowed thirty years ago are still bearing fruit today. He won't be there on her graduation day, but make no mistake about it. His influence opened the door.

Everywhere I go I hear stories about how my father-in-law influenced people's lives. During my last book tour, I was speaking at Allison Park Church in Pittsburgh. The young pastor who picked me up is a fellow graduate of Central Bible College. Not far into our conversation, we discovered that we were from neighboring towns, Naperville and Aurora. I asked him if he'd ever heard of my father-in-law, Bob Schmidgall. He said, "I got the Bob Schmidgall scholarship my senior year at CBC!"

If he hadn't been driving, I would have given him a man hug. Nearly two decades after my father-in-law's death, his seeds of faith are still multiplying. A pastor in Pittsburgh is one of his countless downlines.

Even when you feel as if you aren't making a difference, God might be using you in ways you aren't aware of. And it's not the immediate impact that matters most; it's the exponential impact, to the third and fourth generations.

An inheritance is what you leave *for* someone.

A legacy is what you leave *in* someone.

Go ahead and leave an inheritance, but, more important, leave a legacy. Legacy is the influence your dream has on others even after you die. For some it's short lived. For others, like my father-in-law, influence compounds interest. In fact, they may have more influence in death than they did in life.

Legacy isn't measured by what you accomplish during your life span. Legacy is measured by the lives that are affected by your life long after you are gone.

When King David died, his kingdom was in jeopardy. There had been several coups d'état during his forty-year reign, and there were several more when Solomon assumed the throne. The first threat was posed by Solomon's older brother Adonijah. A second threat was posed by a Benedict Arnold named Joab. In both instances, it was Benaiah that King Solomon commissioned to take care of it.

Benaiah was the linchpin between two generations, two kingdoms.

It was Benaiah's bravery that opened the door of opportunity to become King David's bodyguard. But it was loyalty that opened the door to his inner circle. I can't predict what will earn you the promotion you want, but it won't happen without selfless loyalty. If you want it for the wrong reasons, you're not ready. Until you can selflessly invest yourself in someone else's dream, you're not ready for your own.

Downlines

Tim Scott is the first African American in US history to be elected to both the House of Representatives and the Senate. As a single parent, Tim's mom worked sixteen-hour days just to put food on the table. Too many people growing up in poverty believe their dreams are unattainable and resign themselves to that notion. But for Tim, poverty only strengthened his resolve to both reach his dreams and work to ensure that others do as well.

The genesis of his dream was an eighth grade teacher who spotted political potential and said, "You ought to think about student council." Those seven words changed the trajectory of his life. Never underestimate the power of one well-timed, well-phrased word of encouragement. One sentence can alter someone else's destiny!

I recently met Senator Scott backstage at the Catalyst Next Conference in Washington, DC. During an unplugged interview, the senator said, "I'm a big believer in writing down vision." That's precisely what he did as a nineteen-year-old. Tim's mentor, a Chick-fil-A operator named John Moniz, had a dream of positively influencing one million people. One of those one million was a teenage kid who could only afford fries. John gave Tim free sandwiches and a steady diet of godly wisdom. When John died of a heart attack at thirty-eight, Tim adopted John's dream and one-upped it. He then wrote down that second-generation dream: to positively affect the lives of one *billion* people.

One billion people? That's a five-hundred-pound lion! Especially for a kid who failed English and Spanish. "That doesn't make you bilingual," Tim says in self-deprecating fashion. "It makes you bi-ignorant." But against all odds, Tim is now making decisions that directly affect the lives of 319 million Americans. And those decisions indirectly affect billions around the globe.

In our cultural narrative, Senator Scott is the hero of the story. But Tim would argue that the true hero is an eighth-grade teacher and a Chick-fil-A operator who saw his potential. They are the bylines that helped Tim Scott make headlines. And that's true of Benaiah and his band of brothers.

Every David needs a Benaiah.

Every Tim Scott needs a John Moniz.

And someone needs you!

I'm eternally indebted to the people who have leveraged me—my parents, professors, coaches, mentors, and pastors. Most of their names you would not know—Bob Rhoden, Gordon Anderson, Kirk Hanson, Jac Perrin, Opal Reddin, St. Clair Mitchell, John Green, Michael Smith, Robert Smiley, Dick Foth, Jack Hayford.

Some of my uplines intersected my life for only a few seconds, like a missionary named Michael Smith, who spoke a prophetic word over my life when I was nineteen years old. He wouldn't even remember that moment, but I've never forgotten it. The same is true of Opal Reddin, Jac Perrin, and Gordon Anderson. It was a sequence of conversations with each of them at a critical juncture in my journey that helped me resolve a theological conundrum. Then there is Dick Foth, who has been a spiritual father to me for two decades. The only way I can repay the debt I owe each of them is by doing for others what they have done for me.

Your legacy isn't your dream. Your legacy is leveraging the dreams of those who come after you. Your legacy is your downlines—those you parent, mentor, coach, and disciple. You may not influence a million people, but who knows? You may influence one person who influences a billion people.

The Measuring Stick

One of the greatest miracles in the Bible is Elijah's victory over the five hundred prophets of Baal. Mount Carmel was the high point of his prophetic career, but the turning point was a subtle shift in focus that happened during a season of depression. The tectonic plates shifted when God told Elijah to anoint a successor: "Go, return on your way to the Wilderness of Damascus; and when you arrive, anoint Hazael as king over Syria. Also you shall anoint Jehu the son of Nimshi as king over Israel. And Elisha the son of Shaphat of Abel Meholah you shall anoint as prophet in your place."[5]

Whom are you anointing?

Whom are you setting up for success?

Who's your Hazael, your Jehu, your Elisha?

The true measure of Elijah's success wasn't the fourteen miracles he performed. It was the twenty-eight miracles that Elisha performed after him. Simply put, success is succession. That's how our dreams outlive us. They live on in the second-generation dreams that we inspire. And it's no coincidence that Elisha performed twice as many miracles. God had given him a double portion of Elijah's spirit.

After the death of her husband, President Franklin Delano Roosevelt, Eleanor battled loneliness. In a brilliant biography about Eleanor Roosevelt, *No Ordinary Time*, Doris Kearns Goodwin noted that a verse of poetry given to Eleanor by a friend "inspired her to make the rest of her life worthy of her husband's memory."

One poetic verse was her constant source of encouragement:

They are not dead who live in lives they leave behind. In those
whom they have blessed they live a life again.[6]

My father-in-law died of a heart attack on January 6, 1998, but his
dream is still leveraging mine. He planted Calvary Church in Naperville,
Illinois, and pastored it for thirty-one years. It's his example that inspired my
dream of pastoring one church for life. His heart for missions inspired us to
be a missional church. The mission trips we take and the money we give to
missions are a derivative of his dream—a mission within a mission.

When I stood at the foot of his casket on the day he died, I asked God
for a double portion of his anointing. I wasn't even sure what I was asking
for, but this I know for sure: his dream did not die when he did. His dream
lives on in me, through me. His dream continues to leverage my life in big
ways, in small ways, in strange and mysterious ways. And I want to do the
same for the next generation.

THE RABBIT ROOM

Among the Thirty
2 Samuel 23:24

ON NOVEMBER 25, 1911, a nineteen-year-old Oxford student checked out a small maroon book from the Exeter Reading Room. That book, *A Finnish Grammar* by Sir Charles Eliot, would bore most minds. But to John Ronald Reuel Tolkien, it was a rabbit hole. Tolkien became intoxicated with the Finnish language. He likened it to the discovery of a wine cellar stocked with an exquisite new vintage.[1]

Using Finnish elements, Tolkien created his famed legendarium—a mythological world called Middle-earth. Forty-three years later Tolkien published *The Lord of the Rings*. Voted "Book of the Century" by British bookseller Waterstones, it ranks as the second best-selling novel of all time. Its prequel, *The Hobbit,* ranks third. Together they have sold an estimated 290 million copies. That's a few more than *A Finnish Grammar*!

Like every dream journey, there was a genesis moment. That small maroon book was Tolkien's passport to Middle-earth. And along the way there were defining moments. A hike from Interlaken to Lauterbrunnen, Switzerland, with twelve friends helped Tolkien visualize Bilbo Baggins's epic journey across the Misty Mountains. One line of poetry from a tenth-century Anglo-Saxon poem—"Hail Éarendel, brightest of angels, Sent unto men upon Middle-Earth"[2]—stirred something deep within his soul. And then there was World War I. Trench fever cut short his combat days but not before he befriended butchers, butlers, gardeners, and mail carriers. Tolkien's knack for writing tales about ordinary people with extraordinary courage was inspired by those average Brits, average Bilbos.

Tolkien's dream journey had genesis moments, defining moments. But there is one more piece to the dream puzzle, and it makes all the other pieces fit together. We don't get where God wants us to go by ourselves! If we go it alone, we'll get lost somewhere along the way. Then who's going to pick you up when you fall down? And who's going to push you to your potential?

Misery loves company, and so do dreams. If the presence of company cuts misery in half, then it more than doubles the joy of a shared dream. It's the synergy of shared dreams—the whole is greater than the sum of the parts.

Shortly after writing *In a Pit with a Lion on a Snowy Day*, the tectonic plates shifted in my life. I realized that many of my life goals were selfish in nature, so I edited the list to include others. Life Goal #102 is a good example. Instead of just visiting the Eiffel Tower, I edited my goal and added an element—to kiss my wife at the top of it. That was far more fun!

I then tweaked Life Goals #73, #75, and #80.[3]

I don't just want to bike a century, run a triathlon, or swim the escape from Alcatraz. I want to cross the finish line with one of my kids! Why? Because crossing the finish line all by yourself is half as fun as crossing it with someone else. Or flip the coin. Crossing the finish line with someone you love is twice as fun!

Adding a relational component to my life goals reduced their selfish nature. It was no longer about me, myself, and I. My life goals now leverage others, and that doubles the motivation.

I love the little phrase "among the Thirty." There is something so collegial about this band of brothers. David was the one crowned king, but it was a team effort. Without a team, don't dream very big. But if you rally others to your cause, it's game on!

The Nth Power

They were labeled "a circle of instigators, almost of incendiaries."[4] It would be an apt description of David's mighty men, but those descriptors reference a band of writing brothers called the Inklings. They convened for lunch every Tuesday at The Eagle and Child, a seventeenth-century pub located at 49 St. Giles Street, Oxford, England. It was there, in a private lounge called the Rabbit Room, that they recited their writings to one another.

If those walls could talk!

C. S. Lewis, perhaps the most famous member of the Inklings, once referred to himself as the most reluctant convert in all of Christendom. It was another member of the group, J. R. R. Tolkien, who convinced Lewis of the credibility of Christ. During one of their verbal jousts, Tolkien countered Lewis's intellectual objections with a deathblow to doubt: "Your inability to understand stems from a failure of imagination on your part."[5]

By faith, C. S. Lewis imagined his way to the foot of the cross. He then imagined his Christlike archetype, Aslan, the guardian and savior of a world called Narnia. Lewis's series of seven fantasy novels, *The Chronicles of Narnia,* has sold more than one hundred million copies, landing it not far behind his friend's books on the all-time best-selling book list.

The Inklings shared ideas, dreams, and laughs with one another. "There's no sound I like better," said C. S. Lewis, "than adult male laughter."[6] And there was lots of it!

J. R. R. Tolkien referred to the Inklings as "friendship to the Nth power."[7]

The friendships forged in that Rabbit Room led to a literary revolution unlike anything the world has ever seen. But it wasn't the first revolution forged by friendship.

The Holy Club

More than two hundred years earlier, on that very same Oxford campus, two brothers formed the Holy Club. Members of the club devoted themselves to prayer, study, and friendship. The dynamic duo of John and Charles Wesley founded the Methodist movement, and another member, George Whitefield, became the catalyst for the First Great Awakening in America.

In an individualistic culture like America, we tend to overlook the power of friendship. But friendship is the Nth power. Without a team your dream will fall short of its full potential. Call it a Holy Club. Call it the Inklings. Call it what you want, but it takes a team to accomplish a God-sized dream.

Even Jesus recruited twelve disciples. In some ways the twelve disciples doubled His workload. Their miscues made extra work for Jesus. When Peter cut off the ear of the servant of the high priest, Jesus had to do a miracle just to undo what Peter had done. But Jesus set the example, set the standard.

When we first started National Community Church, I was a one-man band. I answered the phone, folded bulletins, led worship, and preached the sermon. But I quickly realized that our upside potential was awfully low if I did everything. At the beginning of a dream journey, your competency is key. But the longer you lead, the less it's about you. Your potential will be determined by the people you surround yourself with. So hiring decisions become the most important decisions you make because they have an exponential effect.

We take it so seriously that we put every prospective employee through a battery of personality assessments. Why? Because we don't need more people just like me! We need people who can do what I can't.

Our natural tendency is to surround ourselves with people like us. But if you want to grow yourself and your organization, you can't surround yourself with a bunch of yes men and yes women. You need people who think differently and lead differently. That creates a healthy and holy tension, but as with a stringed instrument, tension keeps you in tune. Without tension there is no melody, no harmony.

David was a renaissance man—musician, warrior, poet, and king. But David's greatest gift was identifying giftedness. Where others saw outcasts and misfits, David saw mighty men. First Samuel 22:2 describes them this way: "All those who were in distress or in debt or discontented gathered around him, and he became their commander. About four hundred men were with him." These were not first-round draft picks! Every one of them was from the Island of Misfit Toys. Yet this was the gene pool from which David selected his mighty men.

The description of David's mighty men reminds me a little bit of our early days at National Community Church. When your average attendance is twenty-five people, you need butts in seats! And you'll take anyone you can get. *In distress? Perfect. In debt? No problem! Disgruntled? Discontented? Dysfunctional? Come on in!* We were so desperate for bodies during our church-planting days that we were tempted to use the blow-up dummies that people put in their cars to drive illegally in the HOV lanes!

The Company of Dreamers

If you want to dream bigger dreams, get around dreamers.

It's a subplot in the storyline, but Benaiah was surrounded by dreamers. Some of his exploits were undoubtedly inspired by the exploits of his compatriots. I'm sure some of those heroic deeds were motivated by unsanctified competitive streaks that drove them to one-up each other.

The mighty men had egos just as we do and lots of testosterone as well. But they also pushed each other in a healthy and holy way. When your friend Eleazar, the son of Dodai, fights until his fist freezes to his sword, all excuses are out the window! It pushes you to push yourself.

Who's pushing you?

If you want to get better at any sport, you have to play with someone who is better than you are. In other words, you have to be willing to lose to win. In much the same way, if you want to grow spiritually, you have to be around people who have more faith, more wisdom. Their God-sized dreams will stretch your faith.

I recently spent two days with Dave Ramsey and thirty pastors from across the country talking about stewardship. Dave asked two pastors to speak—Robert Morris, the pastor of Gateway Church in Dallas, Texas, and Craig Groeschel, the pastor of Life Church in Oklahoma City, Oklahoma.

Before Robert spoke, I thought I was generous. Before Craig spoke, I thought I was a visionary. Not compared to them I'm not! And that's precisely why I love being around people like them—they stretch me.

Bob Goff is the author of *Love Does* and an all-around great guy. We sat down to dinner a few years ago, and Bob said, "You guys should take over a country." I was just getting to know Bob, so I thought he was joking. But the expression on his face didn't change. That's when I realized that Bob was serious. And why wouldn't he be? As the honorary consul for the Republic of Uganda, Bob is changing a nation with his courageous fight for justice.

I need to be around people who make me feel small because their dreams are so big. I need to be around people who make me feel far from God because they're so close to Jesus. I need to be around people who make me feel as if I'm doing next to nothing because they're making such a big difference.

We offer a yearlong internship at National Community Church that we call our protégé program. It's unpaid, so protégés raise funds to come work at NCC. It's our farm system. If someone is willing to work for free, it might be someone you want to hire. More than a dozen staff members are former protégés.

Our protégés have a portfolio, and we take them through a rigorous course of leadership development. But it's about more than the job they do or the things they learn. It's about breathing our air, drinking our water. NCC is a dream factory. We invite people into the corporate dream God has given us, and they invite us into the individual dream God has given them. That's our two-step, our dream dance.

When Solomon coined the phrase "iron sharpens iron," I bet he was thinking about David's mighty men. I bet David told bedtime stories about Josheb, Eleazar, and Benaiah. Solomon undoubtedly asked for *the lion story* more than once. And perhaps that story was the seed that led Solomon to appoint Benaiah as his right-hand man after his father's death. It wasn't just a wise choice; it honored the memory of his father. If his father could trust

Benaiah to be his bodyguard, Solomon could trust Benaiah to be his commander in chief.

Three-Part Harmony

I was having lunch with a DC legend, Doug Coe, a few years ago. Few people have had more influence behind the scenes in Washington, DC, over the past half century, and he's done it through relationships. One of Doug's habits is giving pop quizzes during the course of conversations. So Doug asked me if I knew who wrote the epistles to the Thessalonians. I detected from the tone of his voice that it was a trick question, but I said "Paul" anyway. I have three graduate degrees from seminary, so I'm embarrassed to admit that I was wrong. Perhaps it's our individualist bias that causes us to overlook the fact that there are three citations: Paul, Silas, and Timothy.

We read right past it, but the epistle to the Thessalonians is three-part harmony. There are three sets of fingerprints, three anointings on that epistle. Paul may have played first chair, but it wasn't a solo.

Everything God does through you is a testimony to those who have parented you, mentored you, discipled you, coached you, and loved you. You are their downline, and they are your upline.

This number is a guesstimate, but I'm 17.2 percent Dick Foth. When I was a twenty-something pastor with zero experience, he took me under his wing. And he's been a spiritual father to me ever since. It's almost scary how often I find myself thinking like Foth, talking like Foth.

Whether it's a Holy Club, a literary club like the Inklings, or a band of brothers like David's mighty men, you will ultimately reflect those with whom you surround yourself. And they will reflect you. Bad company corrupts good character,[8] but good company helps you go from good to great.

The true test of greatness isn't measured by your accomplishments. The true test of greatness is measured by the accomplishments of those you surround yourself with, those who come after you.

Again, success is succession.
That's how our dreams outlive us.

Pass the Baton

One of my proudest accomplishments is a track-and-field record that still stands at Madison Junior High School in Naperville, Illinois. I was one-fourth of the 4 x 100-meter relay team whose record time has stood for more than thirty years! Unfortunately we lost the city championship because I dropped the baton on the second leg. It's one of my more painful athletic memories.

Someday I'll hand off the lead pastor role of National Community Church, and when I do, I don't want to drop the baton. I want to hand it off, and then I want to run in the same lane right behind whomever I hand it to, cheering that person on for as long as I can keep up!

The greatest badge of honor for Benaiah isn't the fact that he chased a lion or killed two mighty Moabites. It's the fact that he stayed loyal to Solomon when David died. Benaiah was the linchpin between David and Solomon's administrations. Without him the baton would have been dropped and Solomon would have been disqualified. When others committed treason, Benaiah stayed loyal to the royal. It was his integrity, not his bravery, that landed him his second dream job.

This may come as a mild surprise, especially in a book about pursuing dreams, but I don't believe that everybody is destined to pursue his or her own dreams. Not everybody is a maverick dreamer. But if you're not, it's imperative that you get around someone who is. Why? Because without a vision the people perish!

Some people are destined to play second fiddle, but you can still play "The Devil Went Down to Georgia"! Serving someone else's dream isn't less significant than pursuing your own. In my opinion it's more noble. It's the dreamer who gets most of the credit at the curtain call. But I wonder if second fiddles will get most of the reward. And ultimately, it's God who gets all the glory when the final credits roll.

COUNTERNARRATIVES

Benaiah the Pirathonite

2 Samuel 23:30

A HUNDRED YEARS AGO Booker T. Washington was perhaps the most famous black man on the planet. He once shared a spot of tea with the queen of England. He was also the first black man invited to dine with the president at the White House. "To a very extraordinary degree," said President Teddy Roosevelt, "he combined humility and dignity." Then Roosevelt paid him perhaps the highest compliment any person can be paid: "As much as any man I've ever met, he lived up to Micah's verse, 'What more doth the Lord require of thee than to do justice and love mercy and walk humbly with thy God.'"[1]

That's high praise from the president of the United States.

On March 12, 1911, Booker T. Washington was in Des Moines, Iowa, delivering several sermons and speeches on the same day. He spoke to standing-room-only crowds at St. Paul's Episcopal Church, Plymouth Church, Foster's Opera House, and a gathering of four African American churches.[2] Booker T. was the talk of the town.

Later that day Washington was in the lobby of the hotel where he was staying when a white woman mistook him for hotel staff. She asked him for a glass of water, and instead of correcting her or identifying himself, he obliged. He got a glass of water, handed it to her, and asked, "Is there anything else I can get for you?"[3]

That one encounter encapsulates his character. Booker T. Washington was an advisor to presidents, but more important, he was a humble servant.

Fame

We live in a culture that aims at fifteen minutes of fame. We aim too low! Why aim at fame and fortune when eternal reward is on the table? I live in a city where every good deed seems to get a press release or a press conference, but Jesus red-flagged publicity stunts in the Sermon on the Mount: "Be careful not to practice your righteousness in front of others to be seen by them. If you do, you will have no reward from your Father in heaven. So when you give to the needy, do not announce it with trumpets, as the hypocrites do."[4]

Everyone knows the name Bill Gates, the founder of Microsoft, and Warren Buffett, the "Oracle of Omaha." They rank as two of the wealthiest billionaires in the world. But have you ever heard of Chuck Feeney? That's the man Gates and Buffett identify as their hero. Buffett goes so far as to say, "He should be everyone's hero."[5]

Forbes magazine dubbed Chuck Feeney "the James Bond of philanthropy." Like a modern-day Saint Nicholas, the fourth-century bishop of Myra who would don a disguise and secretly give away gifts to the poor, for the last thirty years Feeney has "crisscrossed the globe conducting a clandestine operation to give away a $7.5 billion fortune." His goal? To die broke! Feeney even sounds a little like Old Saint Nick: "People used to ask me how I got my jollies, and I guess I'm happy when what I'm doing is helping people and unhappy when what I'm doing isn't helping people."[6]

God-given dreams are more about others than they are about you. Selfish dreams always short-circuit, but dreams that involve and excite everyone else have a long tail.

There is a fine line between "Thy kingdom come" and "my kingdom come." Ultimately, the goal of a God-given dream is to honor the God who gave it to you in the first place. A God-given dream doesn't go after an earthly award. It aims at the eternal reward Jesus promised right after He red-flagged hypocrisy: "Do not let your left hand know what your right hand is doing, so that your giving may be in secret. Then your Father, who sees what is done in secret, will reward you."[7]

Are you living for the applause of people or the applause of nail-scarred hands? Are you trying to make a name for yourself or make the name of Jesus famous? Are you building altars to God or monuments to yourself?

There are thirty-seven mighty men listed in 2 Samuel 23. Pick a name, any name. I chose Benaiah the Pirathonite because he shares the same first name as Benaiah son of Jehoiada. Maybe they called him Ben to differentiate. I can say with a high level of confidence that Ben wasn't about Ben. He was about David. He wasn't trying to make a name for himself or establish his own throne.

Every mighty man, to a man, risked life and limb for David. Each one's energies were devoted to helping David fulfill his dream.

I've met lots of amazing leaders over the years, and lots of them are amazing people too. But some of them are amazing only from a distance. They're the ones whose egos barely fit through the doorframe. Can I tell you who impresses me most? Those who try to impress the least. Nothing is more impressive than a down-to-earth dreamer who understands that leadership is first and foremost servanthood.

Is your dream about you? Or is it about others?

If your dream is about you, no one will rally around it.

If your dream is about others, you won't be able to keep people away.

Bittersweet

I have the privilege of serving on the board of the Bittersweet Foundation, based in Washington, DC. The executive director, Kate Schmidgall, was recognized by the DC Chamber of Commerce as Young Entrepreneur of the Year in 2014. Kate is a visionary leader, but what I respect most about Kate is that she is all about everyone else.

Fourteen years ago a conviction was conceived in her spirit that the church needs to do a better job of telling stories about a good God who is at work in the world. In Kate's words, "It's an injustice not to." For seven years the dream was nothing more than a desire. If you've ever had a dream that has gathered dust on the shelf, you know that feeling of frustration. Then came the moment of truth. "I knew that I was no longer waiting for God," Kate said. "I knew that God was waiting for me." So Kate chased her lion!

The mission of Bittersweet is sharing counternarratives.

Listen to any twenty-four-hour news cycle, and most of the news is bad. It's not only depressing; it's deceiving. Bittersweet believes that God is not dead, the church is not idle, and faith is not futile. But it's our job, as a story shop, to celebrate those stories! Each month we highlight an inspiring story of a good God at work in the world. If you need a little dose of inspiration, check out the story inventory at bittersweetmonthly.com.

In Luke's gospel there is a common refrain: "The kingdom of heaven is like . . ." And you can fill in the blank with any number of parables. It's like leaven; it's like a mustard seed; it's like a treasure hidden in a field.

Bittersweet believes that the kingdom of heaven is like an eighty-year-old Palestinian woman, Ms. Lydia, who started the Peace Center for the Blind in East Jerusalem. Why did she do it? Because Ms. Lydia is blind herself. We believe the kingdom of heaven is like a master craftsman who uses the tools of his trade to build braces so that kids with polio can go to school, play soccer, dance, and dream. We believe the kingdom of heaven is like DC127, a nonprofit that is rallying churches to reverse the foster-care list in Washington, DC, so there are more families waiting for children than children waiting for families.

How do we push back the kingdom of darkness? By highlighting stories of God's goodness, God's grace. And after we tell the stories, the creative collateral belongs to the organizations we profile so they can share their story with as many people as possible.

We should do what we do for an audience of One, but I also believe that the good news should make the news. We should be making such a huge difference in our communities that we're unignorable.

Like any dreamer, Kate wrestles with doubt—*Does it really make a difference?* Her honest answer: "It's hard for us to know." So why keep going? The short answer is conviction. Have you ever felt so convicted about a cause that you can't *not* do something about it? It's like the prophet Ezekiel, who had fire shut up in his bones![8] "If Bittersweet helps even one person learn to see God in the dark," Kate says, "then I consider it worth my everyday living."

Third Wheel

On bad days I bet Benaiah the Pirathonite felt as if he was second string or a third wheel. After all, he wasn't even the most famous Benaiah in David's band of brothers. I bet he had to repeatedly correct people who mistakenly thought he was the Benaiah who chased the lion. *No, that was Benaiah son of Jehoiada.*

It's hard to get inside the head of someone who lived thousands of years ago, but human nature is human nature. I'm guessing Benaiah the Pirathonite wrestled with self-worth like the rest of us. Some days he felt like a no name. And that causes a wide variety of emotional issues if you're trying to make a name for yourself. But if your dream is about others, it doesn't matter!

My friend Mark Moore leads a wonderful organization called MANA, whose mission is fighting world hunger, one child at a time.[9] Their weapon? Mother Administered Nutritive Aid—packets of peanut butter infused with nutrients that help millions of malnourished kids around the world. Part of what I love about this field-of-dreams story is that their factory in Georgia was built on a field where peanuts used to grow! Another reason I love MANA is because it was launched at Ebenezers coffeehouse on World Hunger Day, 2010. So it feels like a dream within a dream.

If you were to visit MANA headquarters, the first thing you'd notice is the picture of a gaunt Ethiopian girl right inside the entrance. It's a setup. Mark anticipated the question people would ask: "Who's the girl?" I love Mark's answer: "She's the boss!"

MANA isn't about Mark. It's about the millions of nameless, faceless children who deserve a fighting chance. That's why Mark is chasing this five-hundred-pound lion.

The mighty men pledged their fame and fortunes to what seemed to be a lost cause at the time, a fugitive named David. They knew David would get the glory, and they were okay with that. Why? Because David's dream was their dream.

I love the way the Bible doesn't even name some of its heroes, like the widow who gave two mites or the boy who gave his brown-bag lunch to Jesus. It'll be fun to discover their names when everyone is introduced at the Marriage Supper of the Lamb! Of course, your real name isn't the name given to you by your birth parents. It's the name that will be given to you by the Son of God Himself: "To the one who is victorious, I will give some of the hidden manna. I will also give that person a white stone with a new name written on it, known only to the one who receives it."[10]

One of the greatest moments in all eternity will be the moment Jesus pronounces your new name, your true name. When it hits your eardrum, fires across your synapses, and registers in your auditory cortex, it'll be as though your entire life is flashing before your eyes. In that one moment your entire existence will come into perfect focus. That name will unveil your true identity, your true destiny. It will make everything make sense.

Turtle on a Fence Post

One of the perks of living in Washington, DC, is all the memorials and monuments in our backyard. I love the Lincoln Memorial at sunrise, the Jefferson Memorial when the cherry blossoms bud, and the Einstein Memorial off Constitution Avenue because no one knows it exists. That said, no memorial is more emotive than the Vietnam Veterans Memorial. Name after name after name is etched into the black gabbro wall that stretches 246 feet in length.

If you don't know any of the names on the wall, you might be able to make it from one end to the other without crying. But to children and spouses and parents, those names are more than names. Each name represents a universe of emotions, a lifetime of memories.

In one sense, reading the list of thirty-seven names in 2 Samuel 23 is about as exciting as reading the phone book. It's a long list of names we can barely pronounce. To us it's a bunch of no names. But to David it was the band of brothers he went to war with. And without them David would never have become king.

David's greatest talent may have been attracting talent.

Alex Haley, the Pulitzer Prize–winning author of *Roots,* is said to have hung in his office a painting of a turtle sitting on a fence post. "Anytime you see a turtle up on top of a fence post," Haley said, "you know he had some help."[11]

Coaching legend Vince Lombardi said something similar: "The man on top of the mountain didn't fall there."[12]

Whether it's a man on a mountain, a turtle on a fence post, or a king on a throne, you know they had some help getting there. It's true of every dream, every dreamer.

As National Community Church grows larger and larger, I know less and less about more and more. Organizationally, it's too complex to keep a pulse on everything. In other words, my dream outgrew me a long time ago! It takes nearly five hundred volunteers to pull off a weekend at our eight campuses. And we have a dream team that does it week in and week out.

If you are big enough for your dream, your dream isn't big enough for God.

You need a dream that necessitates thirty-seven mighty men, mighty women.

You need a dream that takes dollars and decades.

You need a dream that scares you!

THE THIRTEENTH
VIRTUE

Naharai the Beerothite, the armor-bearer of Joab son of Zeruiah

2 Samuel 23:37

WHEN JOSIAH FRANKLIN DIED on January 16, 1745, his son Benjamin instructed a memorialist to inscribe a verse of Scripture on his father's tombstone. It was his father's favorite proverb: "Seest thou a man diligent in his business? he shall stand before kings."[1]

I don't know why Josiah Franklin staked claim to that particular proverb, that particular promise. Perhaps it was a promise for the next generation of Franklins? Josiah would never stand before a king himself, but he raised a son who would. He dedicated his tenth son to the Lord as a tithe. His dream for Benjamin was that he would become a minister, but instead he became a minister plenipotentiary.

Perhaps the most important diplomat in American history, Benjamin Josiah Franklin secured the support of France during America's struggle for independence. Without his statecraft the American Revolution likely would have failed. And the same could be said for the Continental Congress.

Toward the end of his illustrious and industrious life, Benjamin Franklin made this wide-angle observation: "I did not think that I should ever literally stand before kings, which, however, has since happened; for I have stood before five, and even had the honor of sitting down with one, the King of Denmark, to dinner."[2]

Benjamin Franklin's curriculum vitae might be unmatched among our Founding Fathers. Franklin not only signed the Declaration of Independence but also edited it. His inventions include the lightning rod, the Franklin stove, and bifocals. His periodical, *Poor Richard's Almanac*, made him the most widely read writer in eighteenth-century America. He started the American Philosophical Society, served as postmaster of Philadelphia, and was unanimously elected sixth president of the Supreme Executive Council of Pennsylvania.

A résumé like that can seem a little surreal, but I left out one critical piece of the puzzle. It's not insignificant that Benjamin Franklin served as a clerk in the Pennsylvania General Assembly for fifteen years before he won a seat. He transcribed thousands of speeches before he delivered one. He listened to thousands of debates before he got into one. Benjamin Franklin also served for nearly a decade as an apprentice printer to his brother.

Simply put, he was an understudy. And he studied hard.

We don't know much about Naharai the Beerothite, but we know enough. He was an armorbearer, which means that he carried Joab's armor and ran his errands. It wasn't glamorous work, but it put him in proximity to Joab, who was in proximity to David. And Naharai must have been diligent in his calling, because he is counted among the mighty men. Like each of them, Naharai stood before King David, fulfilling the ancient proverb before David's son Solomon even wrote it. I wouldn't be surprised if King Solomon had the mighty men in mind when he penned those words.

Aide-de-Camp

There is a trend in Scripture that is unignorable. Many of the greatest leaders were understudies. Elisha carried Elijah's mantle. Joshua climbed Mount Sinai with Moses. Even David served as Saul's armorbearer until Saul started throwing spears at him!

What's true in Scripture is true in history.

You may know that our first secretary of the treasury, Alexander Ham-

ilton, served as George Washington's aide-de-camp during the Revolutionary War. But did you know that General Washington had thirty-three
aides? And they are a veritable who's who list in their own right. They didn't
just serve George Washington; they learned how to lead from him.[3]

Edmund Jennings Randolph became the first attorney general of the
United States, as well as the second secretary of state. Jonathan Trumbull Jr.
was elected to the First Congress and served as Speaker of the House in the
Second Congress. Dr. David Cobb was elected to the Third Congress in
1793. Alexander Contee Hanson served in the Senate. David Humphreys
served as foreign minister to both Portugal and Spain. James McHenry had
a fort named after him, and it was the defense of that fort in the Battle of
1812 that inspired Francis Scott Key's "The Star-Spangled Banner." And
last but not least, John Trumball's painting *The Declaration of Independence* graces the back of the two-dollar bill.

I have no idea what Peregrine Fitzhugh, Hodijah Baylies, or Dr. Ebenezer Man went on to do after serving under Washington, but I love their
names. Plus, they remind me of Naharai the Beerothite. Each of Washington's aides-de-camp played a critical role at a critical time in our history,
just like each of David's mighty men.

There is a season to go after your dreams, but there is also a season to
serve someone else's dream. The best way to learn leadership is to serve
under a gifted leader. Washington's aides-de-camp learned things that
couldn't be taught in a classroom. They could be learned only on a battlefield. And the same could be said of David's mighty men.

I live by a little mantra: *Don't seek opportunity; seek God, and opportunity will seek you.* I'm not suggesting that you don't keep your eyes open or
put your best foot forward. And if opportunity knocks, answer it. But the
best path to your dream isn't seeking a position of leadership; it's posturing
yourself as a servant.

All dreamers have to pay their dues, and I fear for those who don't.
Someday you'll owe back taxes for the shortcuts you take. And your success
will be short lived. Don't be in such a hurry to begin the next chapter of

your life that you fail to ace the lessons the current chapter is trying to teach
you.

If you're diligent, you'll stand before kings. Or sit at tables with former
presidents!

How'd I Get Here?

In the past few years, I've had a few *How'd I get here?* moments. I keep
finding myself at tables with people that I have no business being in the
same room with, including lunch with a former president and dinner with
a former NFL MVP. But I've discovered on this dream journey that when
you follow Jesus, you go places that are off the grid and meet people who are
out of your league.

A year ago I was sitting at a table with a three-star general, another
former NFL MVP, and a member of Congress. What did we have in common? We're friends with Dick Foth, of course. I've come to think of it as
the five degrees of Dick Foth! At the head of this table was Dick's former
aide-de-camp Jeremy Vallerand.

As a twenty-something, Jeremy spent a year in DC driving Dick Foth
all over Capitol Hill. He's one of a half-dozen aides who spent a year with
Dick during his time in DC. In fact, Dick's first aide was my brother-in-law
Joel Schmidgall, who now serves as our executive pastor at National Community Church.

During his year in DC, Jeremy became proficient at handling rush-
hour traffic and parallel parking. He also learned invaluable lessons in leadership from Dr. Foth. Fast-forward a decade, and Jeremy now leads an
amazing nonprofit called Rescue:Freedom whose five-hundred-pound lion
is human trafficking.

"What motivates me is the fact that we are able to help boys and girls
escape from slavery," Jeremy said in a recent *Forbes* profile. "Watching them
pursue their dreams is what keeps me going."[4]

Jeremy is a modern-day Moses. His dream is setting slaves free so they can dream again. And to those who run the brothels and work camps, Rescue:Freedom says, "Let my people go!"

Climb for Captives

The genesis moment for Jeremy was his first trip to Kamathipura, which has one of the largest red-light districts in Asia. It was there that Jeremy met thirty-five children who were HIV-positive. He braced himself for what he thought would be a very somber place, but instead he felt as though he had found the fountain of hope. Human trafficking was no longer just an issue; it now had a face. And when Jeremy flew back to his home in Seattle, he left his heart behind.

A few months later Jeremy was planning to climb Mount Rainier on July Fourth. He was going to do it for fun, but then he had an idea. "People do all kinds of things to raise money for causes," Jeremy said. "If you can run marathons for cancer research or sell cookies for Girl Scouts, why can't you climb mountains to rescue kids from slavery?" Especially on the Fourth of July!

Jeremy's goal for that first Climb for Captives was to raise $14,410— one dollar for every vertical foot of the mountain. That first climb raised $20,000, and subsequent climbs have raised $486,000. And Jeremy's dream has caused a chain reaction. "We've seen people use bike races, marathons, dinner parties, garage sales, wedding gifts, dance performances, and micro-roasted coffee," said Jeremy.

People are leveraging what they love to do for the cause they care about.

"I started off by dedicating a climb to a cause," Jeremy said. "Somewhere along the way I dedicated my life to a dream."

When Jeremy moved to Washington, DC, a decade ago, he had no idea what would come of it. And he wasn't sure what he wanted to do with his life. If you're in a similar situation, get around someone with a dream. Get as close as you can. It might just start a chain reaction that changes your life and theirs.

One fun ripple effect: Dick Foth serves as the chairman of the Rescue:Freedom board that Jeremy Vallerand, his former protégé, leads. It's more than a favor to a former aide-de-camp. It's a cause that Dick has devoted the rest of his life to!

Stoop, Young Man

When he was a young man, Benjamin Franklin was quite scathing in his editorials, more than a few of which targeted the Puritan preacher Cotton Mather. In a rather magnanimous gesture, Mather invited Benjamin over for dinner one night and showed him his library. Franklin spent much of his time and money as a young man acquiring one of the largest libraries in America, consisting of 4,276 volumes.

As they walked through a narrow passage into the library, Mather yelled back at Franklin, "Stoop! Stoop!" Franklin didn't understand the exhortation until it was too late and bumped his head on a low beam. Like any good preacher, Mather turned it into a sermon. "Let this be a caution to you not always to hold your head so high. Stoop, young man, stoop—as you go through this world—and you'll miss many hard thumps."

Many years later Franklin told Mather's son that he never forget that moment, that lesson. "This advice, thus beat into my head, has frequently been of use to me," said Franklin, "and I often think of it when I see pride mortified and misfortunes brought upon people by carrying their heads too high."[5]

One of the defining moments of my life was getting cut down to size by a summer intern. I made a prideful statement about National Community Church, and he called me on it. At first I was defensive. But I'm so grateful he had the courage to call me out. I certainly don't want to give the impression that I've conquered pride. Like each of the seven deadly sins, pride has nine lives. You have to fight the battle every single day, but there are decisive victories. And that was one of them.

It was that humbling experience that gave birth to a little mantra that we repeat around NCC all the time: *If you stay humble and stay hungry, there is nothing God cannot do in you or through you.*

Let me pull back the curtain on NCC a little bit. We have an all-star team that is incredibly talented. Our worship leaders are song-writing machines. In my humble opinion, pun intended, they are writing some of the best worship music in America.[6] Our media team produces trailers, documentaries, and short films that are Hollywood quality. And with the help of our friends at Orange,[7] Crosswalk Kids is crushing it. But attitude trumps talent seven days a week and twice on Sunday!

When we hire people, we're certainly looking for skills, for smarts. If you graduated summa cum laude, it tells me you have a head on your shoulders. If you graduated *thank the laude,* we probably won't hire you in our finance department. But even more than aptitude, we're looking for an attitude. We're looking for humility, teachability, and a sense of humor.

At twenty years of age, Franklin identified the virtues that he would diligently work to develop. He created a checklist and graded himself every day. Originally, the list was composed of twelve virtues. It wasn't until he had been humbled a time or two that Franklin added the thirteenth virtue, humility. Next to it he wrote, "Imitate Jesus and Socrates."

There is a sequence in Scripture that is sacrosanct: "Pride goeth before destruction," and "humility comes before honor."[8] In the spiritual order of things, it's inviolable.

Pride is the first chapter in the book of failure.

Humility is the first chapter in the book of success.

God won't put you in a position of leadership until you take a posture of servanthood.

The highest compliment paid to Benaiah may be this one: "He was held in greater honor than any of the Thirty."[9] It's a simple descriptor, but it says so much about Benaiah. Here's my translation: He was *more humble* than any of the Thirty. That's not an exegetical jump; it's a spiritual law. Even if the word *humility* is not explicitly mentioned in the text of Scripture, it's part of the sequence.

And there are two ways to get it: humble yourself or let God humble you. It's one or the other. Choose the former so you don't have to experience the latter!

Humility is the prologue to every success story in Scripture.

It was true of Benaiah.

It was true of Naharai.

It's true of you.

A HUNDRED YEARS
FROM NOW

There were thirty-seven in all.

2 Samuel 23:39

ON DECEMBER 31, 1759, Arthur Guinness opened a brewery in Dublin, Ireland, leasing a four-acre piece of property at St. James Gate. As the western entrance to the city, it had great foot traffic. It was also the site of an annual fair where the best-selling item was ale. But Guinness didn't choose it for those reasons. He knew that city planners intended to build Ireland's Grand Canal adjacent to St. James Gate, which would give his brewery a built-in shipping lane right in its backyard.

Guinness had an eye for opportunity, and he must have had a knack for negotiation too, because he managed to secure a nine-thousand-year lease. You read that right, a nine-thousand-year lease! That must be a Guinness World Record, pun intended.[1] Arthur Guinness put down one hundred pounds and agreed to pay forty-five pounds per annum.

I have no idea why Arthur proposed a nine-thousand-year timeline versus eight thousand or ten thousand. But he was obviously in it for the long haul. Guinness, which is older than America, has a traditional policy that has guided their decision making for 257 years—*considering long and acting quickly.*[2]

That dual-edged philosophy is a good rule of thumb in both business and warfare. Before joining David's ranks, the mighty men undoubtedly did some scenario analysis. If you are part of a coup d'état that fails, it's not just the leader who loses his head. Joining David's band of brothers was a dangerous decision, so I'm sure they thought long and hard about it. But once the decision was made, they acted quickly. After all, it took catlike reflexes for Benaiah to outsmart and outfight that lion!

Considering long.

One of the biggest mistakes we make is thinking in terms of one generation. It's not only shortsighted; it's also selfish. We think that what God does for us is *for us*. And it is, but it isn't. It's also for the third and fourth generations.

We think right here, right now.

God is thinking nations and generations.

The key to dreaming big is *thinking long*. And the bigger the dream, the longer the timeline. If you're thinking in terms of eternity, you should have some dreams that can't be accomplished in your lifetime.

Unborn Millions

Before the Battle of Long Island, General George Washington reminded his troops whom they were fighting for. It wasn't just for their freedom as first-generation Americans. "The fate of unborn millions will now depend, under God, on the courage and conduct of this army."[3]

One hundred fifty years later Abraham Lincoln was trying to get the Thirteenth Amendment, which would abolish slavery, through Congress. Two votes short, Lincoln appealed to the Republican caucus: "The abolition of slavery by constitutional provision settles the fate, for all . . . time, not only of the millions now in bondage, but of unborn millions to come—a measure of such importance that *those two votes must be procured*."[4]

Unborn millions.

Washington and Lincoln had their eyes on the third and fourth generations. That's who they were fighting for. Their dream wasn't about them. It was about the next generation and the generation after that.

Just as Washington and Lincoln were fighting for the next generation of Americans, David and his mighty men were fighting for the next generation of Jews. A kingdom hung in the balance. I can hear David inspiring his men with the same words George Washington used to inspire the Continental army: "We have, therefore, to resolve to conquer, or to die."[5]

Like our Founding Fathers, David's mighty men mutually pledged their lives, their fortunes, and their sacred honor to their cause, their calling. And the rest is history. Their heroic deeds are long remembered, long considered.

What are you doing today that will make a difference one hundred years from now?

Every generation must steward what's been entrusted to them. It starts with honoring the generation that has gone before us by learning everything we can from them. But that's only half the equation when it comes to passing along a generational blessing. It continues by empowering the generation that comes after us. That's how the baton of blessing is passed to the third and fourth generation. And that is what the psalmist advocated in Psalm 78:

So the next generation would know them,
even the children yet to be born,
and they in turn would tell their children.[6]

A Single Seed

In 1914 a young preacher named Ben Mahan started preaching on street corners in Jeannette, Pennsylvania. A church was eventually formed and started gathering above a butcher's shop. Five years later, in 1919, the congregation bought their first church building.[7] And a few years later, a sixteen-year-old boy named George Wood gave his heart to Christ after one of Mahan's messages.

In 1932, George and his wife, Elizabeth, felt called to Northwest China as missionaries. They shared the gospel as best they could, and a church was established. Three children were born to them, including their youngest, also called George, on September 1, 1941.

When Christian missionaries were kicked out of the country, the church that the Woods pastored numbered two hundred souls. For many decades the church went underground. When it resurfaced in 1983, one of the Chinese pastors with whom George Wood had worked restarted that congregation with thirty people. When he died in 2004, the church numbered fifteen thousand people!

When asked how it happened, the ninety-six-year-old pastor said, "Jesus Christ is the same yesterday, today, and forever. And we prayed a lot."

Your dream is setting up someone else's dream. You are planting seeds that someone else will harvest, just as you are harvesting seeds that someone else planted. I love the way Stanley Tam said it: "God can't reward Abraham yet because his seed is still multiplying."[8] And the same is true of Ben Mahan, George Wood, and you.

Ben Mahan had no earthly idea when he planted a church in Jeannette, Pennsylvania, that the seeds he sowed would reap a harvest in the Qinghai province of China a hundred years later. But when we plant and water, God gives the increase. And He determines when, where, and how.

Seeds of faith germinate across nations and generations.

I first heard that story from the General Superintendent of the Assemblies of God, George Wood—the son of missionaries George and Elizabeth Wood. In fact, he shared the story not far from the church in Jeannette, Pennsylvania, where his dad got saved. George had recently visited the church and walked the same aisle his father walked when he got saved in 1924.

Just as George Wood inherited his name from his father, his name has been passed down to his son and grandson—four generations of Georges. There are fifty-eight members in their extended family, and fifty-six of them know Jesus Christ as their personal Lord and Savior. I might suggest that each and every one of them is Ben Mahan's downline.

The seed of faith Ben Mahan planted is multiplying across nations—from Jeannette, Pennsylvania, to the Qinghai province. And it's germinating across generations. The Assemblies of God is the fastest-growing movement in the history of Christendom, with sixty-seven million adherents worldwide just a century after it started.

Don't underestimate the power of a single seed.
It has the power to influence nations and generations.

Dream Journal

Every year our staff at NCC goes on two retreats. Our summer retreat is called Pray and Play, and, you guessed it, we pray and play. Our fall retreat is called Pray and Plan. We've done our fall retreat in Baltimore's Inner Harbor fifteen years running now. The by-product of that retreat is a strategic plan. We establish priorities and put timelines to our dreams. Of course, God surprises us every year with things we most definitely didn't plan.

Before our latest retreat I went back and read our strategic plan from a decade earlier. It not only reminded me of how far we've come, but I also saw the seeds of some of the dreams that have come to pass since then.

On October 18, 2015, NCC launched its eighth campus at the largest music venue and dance club in Washington, DC. The Echostage is situated right next to a gentlemen's club and across the street from a marijuana manufacturing plant. And they both let us use their parking lots on Sunday mornings.

Shortly after opening that campus, a car pulled up and asked one of our parking volunteers when the strip club opened. He said, "I'm not sure, but we're having church right now." The two guys in the front seat drove off but not before the girl in the backseat got out of the car and walked into church.

One of our core convictions is that the church belongs in the middle of the marketplace. It's why we meet in movie theaters. It's why we built a coffeehouse. It's why we own and operate a first-rate, second-run movie theater on Capitol Hill. And it's why we meet in a music venue next to a strip club.

Here's what I wrote in our strategic plan a decade before:

> We're called to the middle of the marketplace—right now that
> means meeting in a movie theater. In 2006 it will mean opening a
> coffeehouse where the church and community can cross paths. We
> also need to look to redeem other social spaces like dance clubs.

I have no recollection of writing those words. A dance club? I couldn't even do the Running Man back then! But the seeds of what God is doing now were planted in my spirit a decade before.

A decade ago I was a nervous leader. I was afraid that if we missed it, we would miss it. I failed to appreciate the fact that God does what God does in spite of us, not just because of us. We just need to stay out of the way! God is the One ordaining our days, ordering our footsteps, and preparing good works in advance. And when that's the locus of your confidence, it's not self-confidence. It's holy confidence.

It's an unshakable sense of destiny.

It's a sanctified stubborn streak.

Next to my Bible, nothing is more sacred to me than my journal. I call it a prayer journal, but it doubles as my dream journal. After all, praying is a form of dreaming, and dreaming is a form of praying.

One of my annual rituals is doubling back and rereading my journal. It's my way of making sure I'm learning the lessons God is trying to teach me. It also helps me connect the dots between my prayers and God's answers. My dream journal is the seedbed where God ideas germinate.

One of our eight campuses is the historic Lincoln Theatre, where Duke Ellington and Ella Fitzgerald got their start. If you looked through my journals, you'd find the Lincoln Theatre circled half a dozen times over a span of several years. We dreamed of meeting there long before the door finally opened. If we hadn't nurtured that seed of faith by circling it in prayer, I'm not sure it would be one of our campuses today.

Every dream, no matter how big, starts out as a seed. And like a seed, it often goes underground for a season. That's when we get discouraged because we don't see any physical evidence of the dream's progress. But it has to take root before it can bear fruit.

A Hundred Years from Now

A panoramic picture of the Sun Moon Mountain pass hangs on the wall of George Wood's office as a reminder of the place where he spent the first six years of his life. It's also a reminder of the legacy his missionary parents left him.

Two maxims, repeated by his mother, Elizabeth, are foundational to George's approach to life and ministry. "When we stand before God," his mother said, "He won't ask us if we've been successful. He'll ask us if we've been faithful."

The second maxim was repeated as often as George got upset: "Now, Georgie, it won't matter a hundred years from now."

At different points in my life, I've felt like the dream God has given me is too big for me. And that's because it is. By definition, a God-sized dream is beyond your ability, beyond your resources. If a dream is from God, it will require divine intervention. But I've also learned that sometimes a dream feels as if it's too big for us because it's not just for us!

That's how I felt when we purchased the castle on Capitol Hill for $29.3 million. I didn't have a category for a dream that big. Honestly, I wasn't sure we needed a city block. And maybe we don't. But the next generation might. And that's who we're building it for.

It's not about us.

It's not about now.

Whatever God is doing in us here and now, He's doing for the third and fourth generation. The dream God has given you is the seed of something He wants to do a hundred years from now. You likely won't be around to witness it, but others are going to reap where they haven't sown because of your faithfulness.

I love Elizabeth Wood's maxim "It won't matter a hundred years from now." It's a reminder to zoom out and see the big picture. It's a reminder that one's life will soon be past and only what's done for Christ will last. Don't worry about the things that have zero bearing on eternity! Your only regret at the end of the day will be the time, talent, and treasure you didn't give back to God.

Now let me also flip the maxim: *it will matter a hundred years from now.* No prayer will go unanswered. No sacrifice will go unnoticed. No gift will go unrewarded. Those things will compound interest for all eternity!

Don't give up on your dream. If you do, you aren't just giving up on its present-tense reality. You're giving up on its future-tense potential. Were there moments when we felt like throwing in the towel on National Community Church? Absolutely! Especially during the first two years. But we wouldn't have been giving up on just the hundred people who attended NCC at the time. We would have been forfeiting everything God has done over the last two decades.

Keep dreaming God-sized dreams.

Keep chasing five-hundred-pound lions.

It makes all the difference in the world.

It makes all the difference for eternity.

Before You Were Born

Jonathan Gray grew up in the nation's capital when it was the murder capital of the country. The city is safer now than it was then, but it's still the tale of two cities. As the political epicenter of the free world, it's the epitome of first-world power. But those who live here know that there is also a statistical third-world country in our backyard. Crime and poverty are far too rampant, homelessness and fatherlessness are epidemic, and the HIV rate is higher than in many African nations.

Jonathan grew up in the middle of that mayhem. He dropped out of school in the eighth grade and started down the wrong path. Jonathan didn't go to church, but one day the church came to him. At the age of thirteen, Jonathan gave his life to Christ at a Teen Challenge outreach. Three decades later Jonathan Gray serves as the executive director of that very same ministry.

Jonathan and his wife have raised their three children in the suburbs, but when they turn fourteen, Jonathan has a sacred ritual. He drives them into the city and parks at the corner of Blaine and 50th Street NE. Then he tells them what God did for them *before they were even born.*

"I tell them how I was running the streets, stealing from everyone, and getting into all kinds of trouble," Jonathan says. "Then I tell them how a man brought a church into our neighborhood, set up on a street corner, and starting telling everyone about Jesus."

That street corner is Jonathan's Damascus road. It's the place where Jesus intersected Jonathan's life and Jonathan made a right turn. There are now three generations of Grays following Christ, but each of their spiritual genealogies traces back to that street corner. It wasn't just the turning point of Jonathan's life; it was the turning point for generations yet to be born.

"I tell my children what Christ's coming into my life did for them even before they were born," Jonathan says. "I tell them that the Lord was taking excellent care of them before they were even born."

Your destiny doesn't begin at birth. Before your parents even met, God was setting you up. You were conceived in the mind of God before you were conceived in your mother's womb. And everything God did for them, He was doing for you.

Everything God did for George Wood Sr., he did for George Wood Jr.

Everything God did for Jonathan, he did for Charles, Janelle, and Alana.

And everything God did for David, he did for Solomon.

Your story might not seem as dramatic as Jonathan's, but it's no less providential. Your dream may not seem as historic as David's, but it's no less significant.

Before you were born, God was at work in your life by working in the lives of those who would influence you. And it's not limited to one or two generations. For me it goes back at least six generations.

Last Will and Testament

Until recently I knew very little about my family tree—a few names, a few stories. But it's amazing what you can unearth with a Google search. I discovered a family treasure, a copy of my great-great-great-great-grandfather's will.

Andreas Pannenkuchen was born in Philadelphia County in 1730. At some point his German surname was Americanized to Pancake. And, yes, it's rather ironic that a Batter-son comes from a long line of Pancakes!

On September 11, 1793, Andrew Pancake drafted his last will and testament. He left one black cow to his wife, Elisabeth. He left five pounds to
his oldest son, John, who executed the will. And he left the farm, literally, to
his son Joseph. Then he penned these words: "Being at presant weak in
body but of sound Disposing mind and memory thanks be to god for his
Goodness and mercyes."[9]

I love the allusion to the Twenty-third Psalm. It happens to be one of
my favorite phrases in all of Scripture—"surely goodness and mercy shall
follow me all the days of my life." Coincidentally, it was my grandmother on
the Pancake side of the family that first helped me memorize that psalm.

I got goose bumps when I first read my great-great-great-great-
grandfather's will because I realized that God's goodness and mercy have
been following me for at least six generations!

The word *follow* can also be translated *chase*; in fact, it might be a better translation. Just as Benaiah chased a lion into a pit on a snowy day, God's
goodness and mercy are chasing after you. The Hebrew root, *radaph*, is a
hunting term. The Hound of Heaven is on your tail, on your trail. He
chases us down the corridors of time until the day we repent. Then He
captures us with His goodness and mercy for all eternity.

No matter how far or how long you run away from God, if you turn
around, you'll discover that God has been following you. He's right behind
you with arms open wide, ready to embrace you. My own grandfather is a
testimony to this fact. The only time he used God's name, it was in vain.
But even after a lifetime of running away from God, my grandpa discovered
that God had been running after him. In a hospital room in Forest Lake,
Minnesota, he was captured by the goodness and mercy of God, which had
chased him for seventy-six years!

Thirty-Nine Begats

Most of us know next to nothing about our great-great-grandparents, but
the decisions they made have influenced our lives in innumerable and incalculable ways. If my great-great-grandfather-in-law, Christian Schmidgall,

hadn't immigrated to America in 1902, the landscape of my life would look very different. The same is true of my Swedish ancestors, the Johanssons, who immigrated to America in the nineteenth century.

Our eyes often glaze over when we get to the genealogies in Scripture. They're long lists of names we can't even pronounce. But I've come to appreciate the genealogies as a timeless testimony to God's faithfulness.

Every dream has a genealogy—even the Son of Man, the Son of God, the Son of David. The genealogy of Jesus is recorded in Matthew's gospel. There are forty-two generations, forty-two begats, and, I would submit, forty-two miracles.

A genealogy is a storyline. And the names listed are the cast of characters. In the case of Jesus, there is one plot twist that hyperlinks with 2 Samuel 23: "Jesse begat David the king; and David the king begat Solomon of her that had been the wife of Uriah."[10]

You probably know the storyline but perhaps not the subplot. David committed adultery with Bathsheba. Then he tried to cover it up by having Bathsheba's husband, Uriah the Hittite, killed. You might assume that Uriah was a random soldier in David's army, but he was actually one of David's mighty men. The last name listed in 2 Samuel 23 is Uriah the Hittite. So David used the crown that Uriah helped him secure to betray his marriage and plot against his life.

As messed up as those circumstances were, God still begat the Messiah. Even in the midst of heartbreak, God still begets miracles! And it's not the first or last time.

Remember Rahab?

That one act of kindness generated a ripple effect that resulted in your salvation!

A few years ago we launched an initiative in Washington, DC, called City Fathers. The heart behind it is simple: if we don't honor those who have gone before us, we rob them of the opportunity to bless those who come behind. We live in a culture that prioritizes fifteen minutes of fame higher than a lifetime of faithfulness. It's all about the latest and greatest. So we decided to honor our city fathers and city mothers—those who have been plowing and planting in this harvest field long before we showed up.

At our first event we invited four pastors. The longest tenured pastor was Bishop Alfred Owens, pastor of Greater Mount Calvary Holy Church, who has pastored in this city for half a century. He's pastored in this city longer than I've been alive! The four pastors have cumulatively spent 147 years in ministry in Washington, DC.

My point? I'm reaping where I have not sown! The blessings I've enjoyed are the direct and indirect by-product of the faithfulness of those who have gone before me. Their dreams have leveraged me in ways I won't even be able to imagine until I cross the space-time continuum.

Lion Chaser

We shared only one lunch together, but Dr. Richard Halverson, is a hero of mine. The former senate chaplain sowed seeds in the nation's capital that are still germinating decades after his death. One such seed is the benediction I pronounce at the end of our services at National Community Church. It was inspired by and adapted from his benediction as pastor of Fourth Presbyterian in Bethesda, Maryland.

> When you leave this place you don't leave the presence of God. You
> take the presence of God with you wherever you go.

I've perused many of Dr. Halverson's sermons and prayers, and my personal favorite may be his "old man" speech. And it goes for old women too.

> You're going to meet an old man someday down the road—ten,
> thirty, fifty years from now—waiting there for you. . . . That old
> man will be you. He'll be the composite of everything you do, say,
> and think—today and tomorrow. . . . His heart will be turning out
> what you've been putting into it. Every little thought, every deed
> goes into this old man.

Every day in every way you are becoming more and more like yourself. Amazing but true. You're beginning to look more like yourself, think more like yourself, and talk more like yourself. You're becoming yourself more and more.

I can imagine each of David's mighty men as old men. Their many battles had left their bodies bruised and battered, shells of their former selves. Josheb suffered from bursitis in his shoulders. Eleazar had arthritis in his wrists. And Benaiah could barely bend over because of a slipped disc or two. Their fighting days had taken a toll, but they would pay the price all over again. Not one of them would trade a single day! And no one could take away the dream that became reality during their lifetime—they crowned David king, their legacy for all eternity!

David's mighty men must have felt a little like the soldiers who heard King Henry V's immortal words before the Battle of Agincourt:

> Gentlemen in England now a-bed
> Shall think themselves accurs'd they were not here,
> And hold their manhoods cheap whiles any speaks
> That fought with us upon Saint Crispin's day.[11]

In case you haven't figured it out by now, *Chase the Lion* is not just a book; it's a call to arms! It's okay to pray a hedge of protection around those you love—God is our Refuge, our Shield. But He is also our Banner—the God who goes before us, the God who fights for us!

Jesus didn't die just to keep you *safe*.

He died to make you *dangerous*!

Can I tell you who I think you are? You are a lion chaser!

So do what you were destined to do.

Chase the lion!

DISCUSSION QUESTIONS

Chapter 1—Chase the Lion

1. Mark writes, "You are one idea, one risk, one decision away from a totally different life. . . . It'll probably be the toughest decision you ever make, the scariest risk you ever take. But if your dream doesn't scare you, it's too small" (page 2). What is the first idea that comes to your mind when you think about following a dream?
2. When have you run from something you're afraid of? When have you chased after the wrong thing?
3. In what ways has a fear of making mistakes influenced your choices in life?
4. Who could join you in chasing the lion in your life?
5. What does it mean for you to "play offense" with your life (page 4)?

Chapter 2—A Dream Within a Dream

1. Do you see yourself as a dreamer? Why or why not?
2. What unbelief or false sense of impossibility do you need to repent of?
3. Why is it important for your dream to be beyond your ability?
4. Who has been a prophet in your life? Think back to early childhood as well as recent years.
5. What does it mean to "criticize by creating" (page 16)? When have you seen this happen?

Chapter 3—The Ripple Effect

1. What is an "inciting incident" in your life (page 21)?
2. When has an act of kindness changed your life? What were the ripple effects of that act?
3. When has an act of courage changed your life? What were the ripple effects of that act?
4. Spend some time taking inventory of God's faithfulness in your life

(see page 28). Write down or share with your small group times of God's blessing and generosity to you.

Chapter 4—The Door to the Future

1. Mark writes, "Dreams are highly contagious!" (page 30). If you don't have a dream right now, who is a dreamer you could spend time with?
2. "Many people die long before their heart stops beating. We start dying the day we stop dreaming. And ironically, we start living the day we discover a dream worth dying for" (page 30). Would you say our culture supports this idea? Why or why not?
3. What are some of your favorite Scripture passages? In what ways are they becoming the script of your life (see pages 31–32)?
4. Mark quotes Graham Greene: "There is always one moment in childhood when the door opens and lets the future in" (page 33). What moment in childhood, even if small, would you point to as a time that let in your future dream?
5. Who could you compliment today, recognizing that the ripple effects of one compliment can change the course of someone's life? Who could you "brag about" behind his or her back?

Chapter 5—The Game of Inches

1. When has an apparent mistake or accident changed your life for the good?
2. What closed doors in your life do you now thank God for?
3. Why would God use small conversations and moments to stir His dreams in us?
4. Would you say you are in your dream job now? Why or why not? Either way, in what ways is your current job helping to shape and fulfill your dreams?
5. Describe a "two-inch event" in your life, one in which you almost missed out on something big God had for you, even if you didn't realize it until later (page 39).

Chapter 6—The Decisive Moment

1. Describe a time when you were tempted to let what you couldn't do keep you from doing what you could.
2. In what ways do churches get stuck in "doing church" or "doing missions" in the same way past generations have done them?
3. As you consider the dream you want to chase, in what ways [used just above] do you need to choose your battles wisely (see page 59)?
4. What's the difference between operating in "a spirit of fear" and operating in "a spirit of focus" (page 62)?
5. As you consider chasing your lion, what do you need to start doing today for that to happen? What do you need to stop doing?

Chapter 7—Frozen

1. How do you respond to the idea of needing practice and discipline to achieve your dream?
2. How do a "prayer ethic" and a "work ethic" go together (page 66)?
3. Mark writes about how our culture is focused on "fifteen minutes of fame" rather than a "long obedience in the same direction" (page 69). In what ways do you think that attitude has affected the pursuit of your dreams?
4. What life goals do you have that will take a lifetime to accomplish? What goals do you have that can't be accomplished in a lifetime?
5. Why is celebrating what God has done so important? Why is it more important than focusing on ways we have failed?
6. Has God released you from a previous dream you've had? Are you still holding on to that dream, or have you let it go?

Chapter 8—Field of Dreams

1. When has a change in your routine or a change in setting drawn you closer to God?
2. If you could go back to one place where God has done something significant in your life, where would you go? Why does *place* make such a difference in our lives?

3. Mark writes, "Only when the dream is dead and buried can it be resurrected for God's glory" (page 81). When have you seen this to be true in your own life or in someone else's life?

4. When have you doubted God by doubting yourself?

5. Why do you think we sometimes have to take the first step before God reveals the second step?

Chapter 9—On This Spot

1. Would you say you are actively pursuing your dream today or are you in a holding pattern? Whatever stage of your dream you are in right now, how can you prove your integrity there?

2. Why is it important to share your struggles and losses as well as your victories?

3. How does having an eternal perspective influence the daily actions you take to chase your lion?

4. Why is it important to realize that the dream isn't about you but about God? In what ways does God help you see that?

Chapter 10—The Lion's Den

1. Why might God call you to go into a situation without promising you success?

2. How would you define success in your life?

3. Why is God's will dangerous?

4. In what ways do Christians sometimes promote the idea that success means wealth, health, and prosperity? What does Scripture have to say about that perspective?

5. When are you most likely to equate earthly success with eternal success?

Chapter 11—Fight Club

1. Mark mentions fighting the devil with "words of faith" and "songs of praise" (page 110). How could you do this in your own life right now? What other ways can you fight the devil's attacks today?

2. What practical difference does it make to see yourself as "more than a conqueror" rather than as a victim (pages 111–12)?

3. What does it mean that God is fighting for you?

4. Mark writes, "Until the pain of staying the same becomes more acute than the pain of change, nothing happens" (page 114). Would you say the pain of staying the same or the pain of change seems more dangerous to you in your life today?

5. What's the most foolish thing about your dream (see page 115)?

Chapter 12—Run to the Roar

1. What's the difference between faith and recklessness?

2. Mark says that lion chasers "don't seek safety; they seek situations that scare them to life" (page 125). When have you been scared to life?

3. Would you say you're more afraid of missing opportunities or making mistakes? Why?

4. What are some biblical examples of doing something crazy for the sake of God?

5. Mark says, "You'll never be ready" (page 127). Have you ever used your lack of readiness as an excuse?

Chapter 13—Snowy Day

1. How might God "recycle" suffering, failure, and disappointment in your life for His purposes (page 130)? How have you seen Him do this in the past?

2. What excuses have you made for not chasing your dream that you need to confess?

3. What do you need to start? Consider Mark's suggestion on page 133: write down your start date, which hour in the day you are going to give to God, and your deadline.

4. Do you consider yourself a perfectionist? Why or why not?

5. What is something in your life you could get 80 percent done rather than waiting for when you could do it 100 percent correctly?

Chapter 14—Five-Pound Dream

1. How is your dream dependent on others' dreams? How are others' dreams dependent on yours?
2. How do you usually respond to criticism?
3. When have you experienced opposition to a dream you've had?
4. Does your dream require a financial commitment right now? What would stepping out in faith, financially, look like?
5. What checkpoints could you have to determine whether you are being faithful or dumb in taking a financial risk for the sake of your dream?

Chapter 15—Double Destiny

1. Why do you think God rarely reveals a complete dream and the means to accomplish it all at once?
2. Mark writes, "Everything in your past is preparation for something in your future" (page 149). How do you respond to the idea that God is wasting nothing in your life?
3. What is something in your childhood that God is using today for good—a skill, a teacher's encouragement, a loss, a school assignment, a friendship?
4. What's the difference between a job and a calling?

Chapter 16—Chain Reaction

1. What do you know about previous generations in your family—their beliefs, their countries of origin, their jobs? Has a spiritual faith been passed down to you, or are you (as far as you know) a first-generation believer?
2. What's a little thing you could do in your life right now as if it is a big thing, knowing that "God will do big things like they're little things" (page 156)?
3. What spiritual legacy do you most want to leave to future generations?
4. Think of someone in your life who has influenced you in a positive

way. How can you repay that person by influencing someone else in a
similar way?
5. Who in your life are you helping to set up for success?

Chapter 17—The Rabbit Room

1. Who could you share your dream with this week?
2. Do you find it easy or difficult to ask for help? Why?
3. Who in your life makes you feel small because his or her dreams are
   so big? Does that inspire you or discourage you?
4. Mark writes, "The true test of greatness isn't measured by your
   accomplishments. The true test of greatness is measured by the
   accomplishments of those you surround yourself with, those who
   come after you" (page 171). How does this truth influence your
   actions, words, and dreams?
5. Do you believe you are called to serve your own dream or someone
   else's dream right now? How and why?

Chapter 18—Counternarratives

1. In what ways does culture encourage you to aim low with your life? In
   what ways does the church in America sometimes encourage you to
   aim low?
2. Why do dreams for the sake of others tend to attract more supporters?
   Why do they last longer than self-centered dreams?
3. Do you believe fulfilling a dream should be personally satisfying?
   Why or why not?
4. Are you waiting on God to pursue your dream, or is God waiting on
   you? How do you know?
5. Are you willing to pursue a calling even if you don't know whether it
   will make a difference? Why or why not?

Chapter 19—The Thirteenth Virtue

1. How does pride get in the way of dreams?
2. When have you seen someone serve before he or she became a leader?

3. Who could you serve under or learn from as you pursue your dream?
4. How would you define *ministry*? Do you believe you could be a minister in a secular job as much as in a church or nonprofit ministry position? Why or why not?

Chapter 20—A Hundred Years from Now

1. Marks says thinking only in terms of one generation is selfish (see page 190). Why do you agree or disagree?
2. In what practical ways could you honor previous generations by learning from them?
3. Mark writes, "God does what God does in spite of us, not just because of us" (page 194). How do we "step out of the way" of God's work even as we pursue God's calling?
4. What's the difference between self-confidence and holy confidence?
5. How has *Chase the Lion* changed your view of your dreams? How will you live differently because of this change in perspective?

ACKNOWLEDGMENTS

It takes a team to accomplish a dream, and that's certainly true of *Chase the Lion*. I owe a debt of gratitude to WaterBrook Multnomah for publishing my first book, *In a Pit with a Lion on a Snowy Day*. What a joy to celebrate the ten-year anniversary with a sequel.

Thanks for your vision for this book, Alex. After all our shared meals and conversations over the years, it's wonderful to have a book to show for it! Thanks to Andrew, Carol, Laura, and Julia for your editing eyes! I love this cover as much as any book I've written, so special thanks to Mark Ford. And thanks to Ginia, Chris, Brett, Lori, and Kim for helping get this book into the right hands at the right time.

Thanks to my agent, Esther Fedorkevich. You are the best in the business! And thanks to the entire team at the Fedd Agency—Whitney, Lisa, and the rest of the best.

Thanks to the church I have the privilege of serving as pastor, NCC. I wouldn't want to be anywhere else doing anything else! Thanks to our amazing stewardship team and executive leadership team for the privilege of pastoring and the margin to write. And to our staff, you are an all-star team! Special thanks to Jill Wyman, my executive assistant. And thanks to our pastor of prayer, Heidi Scanlon, and the entire prayer team at NCC for your ceaseless prayers for me.

Finally, thanks to my wife, Lora. I love chasing lions with you! And to my three children—Parker, Summer, and Josiah—the joy of being your father is indescribable. Ten years ago I dedicated *In a Pit* to you. What a joy to watch you grow up and become lion chasers!

NOTES

Chapter 1: Chase the Lion

1. 2 Samuel 23:20, NLT.
2. Janet Jennings, *The Blue and the Gray* (Madison, WI: Cantwell Printing, 1910), 178.
3. See 2 Samuel 23:21.
4. Thanks to Stephen Covey for this metaphor. I first encountered this idea in *The 7 Habits of Highly Effective People*.
5. Matthew 25:21, 23.
6. A little nod to one of my favorite authors, Oswald Chambers. His devotional *My Utmost for His Highest* is an all-time classic.
7. See Ephesians 3:20.

Chapter 2: A Dream Within a Dream

1. David McCullough, *The Wright Brothers* (New York: Simon & Schuster, 2015), 36.
2. See Ephesians 3:20.
3. "Dream Within a Dream," on *The Inception*, Wikia, http://inception .wikia.com/wiki/Dream_Within_A_Dream.
4. Edgar Allan Poe, "A Dream Within a Dream," PoeStories.com, http://poestories.com/read/dreamwithin.
5. Acts 2:17.
6. See 1 Samuel 16:1–13.
7. Loren Cunningham with Janice Rogers, *The Book That Transforms Nations: The Power of the Bible to Change Any Country* (Seattle: YWAM Publishing, 2007), 62.

Chapter 3: The Ripple Effect

1. "Paul Tudor Jones," Wikipedia, last modified February 24, 2016, https://en.wikipedia.org/wiki/Paul_Tudor_Jones.
2. Andy Serwer, "The Legend of Robin Hood," *Fortune,* September 8, 2006.
3. Paul Tudor Jones, quoted in Tony Robbins, *Money: Master the Game* (New York: Simon & Schuster, 2014), 494.
4. See Psalm 127:1.
5. Joshua 2:12.

6. Galatians 6:9–10.
7. "Gerda Weissmann Klein," Wikipedia, last modified April 24, 2016, https://en.wikipedia.org/wiki/Gerda_Weissmann_Klein.
8. "New England Holocaust Memorial," Wikipedia, last modified May 17, 2015, https://en.wikipedia.org/wiki/New_England_Holocaust_Memorial.
9. Leonard Mlodinow, *Subliminal: How Your Unconscious Mind Rules Your Behavior* (New York: Vintage Books, 2013), 46.

Chapter 4: The Door to the Future

1. "Wilson A. Bentley: The Snowflake Man," Snowflake Bentley: The Official Web Site of Wilson A. Bentley, Jericho Historical Society, http://snowflakebentley.com/bio.htm.
2. I count fifty-one question marks in Job 38–39. Of course, some of them contain questions within questions, so the grand total is even more. It's quite the pop quiz!
3. Job 37:14.
4. M. B. Mullet, "The Snowflake Man," *The American Magazine,* February 1925, 29.
5. Jim Cymbala, "What Happens When the Church Prays?" Pray for Revival! May 13, 2013, https://prayforrevival.wordpress.com/category/jim-cymbala/.
6. Steven Furtick, *Sun Stand Still: What Happens When You Dare to Ask God for the Impossible* (Colorado Springs, CO: Multnomah, 2010), 23–24.
7. "Graham Greene," Brainy Quote, www.brainyquote.com/quotes/quotes/g/grahamgree166575.html.
8. Brian Grazer and Charles Fishman, *A Curious Mind: The Secret to a Bigger Life* (New York: Simon & Schuster, 2015), xv.

Chapter 5: The Game of Inches

1. Ed Catmull, *Creativity Inc.: Overcoming the Unseen Forces That Stand in the Way of True Inspiration* (New York: Random House, 2014), 176.
2. Catmull, *Creativity Inc.,* 176.
3. "Quote: Dialogue from Back to the Future, Part II," Wikia, http://backtothefuture.wikia.com/wiki/Quote:Dialogue_from_Back_to_the_Future,_Part_II.
4. "Fun Fact: First Ten Move Possibilities," Chess.com, https://www.chess.com/forum/view/general/fun-fact-first-ten-move-possibilities.

5. Acts 17:28.
6. See Acts 17:26.
7. "Albert Schweitzer Hospital," Wikipedia, last modified December 5, 2015, https://en.wikipedia.org/wiki/Albert_Schweitzer_Hospital.
8. Albert Schweitzer, *Out of My Life and Thought: An Autobiography*, 60th anniv. ed. (Baltimore: Johns Hopkins University Press, 2009), 85–86.
9. Schweitzer, *Out of My Life*, 82.
10. Ben has also written a great book titled *Dream Year*, which I highly recommend.

Chapter 6: The Decisive Moment

1. "Death of Alan Kurdi," Wikipedia, last modified April 26, 2016, https://en.wikipedia.org/wiki/Death_of_Alan_Kurdi.
2. One billion divided by one hundred equals ten million.
3. "Death of Alan Kurdi," Wikipedia.
4. "Henri Cartier-Bresson," Wikipedia, last modified April 5, 2016, https://en.wikipedia.org/wiki/Henri_Cartier-Bresson.
5. Thanks again to my friends at the New Wine Conference for one of the most remarkable weeks of my life. Your hospitality was humbling, and the conference was life changing.
6. Stefan Zweig, *Decisive Moments in History: Twelve Historical Miniatures* (Riverside, CA: Ariadne Press, 1999), 5.
7. Although the quote is generally attributed to Burke, the source is uncertain.
8. Julia Ward Howe, "The Battle Hymn of the Republic," http://special needsinmusic.com/folk_song_pages/battle_hymn.html.
9. "Elizabeth Fry," Wikipedia, https://en.wikipedia.org/wiki/Elizabeth_Fry.
10. David Wills, Terry Parker, and Greg Sperry, *Family. Money: Five Questions Every Family Should Ask About Wealth* (Alpharetta, GA: The National Christian Foundation, 2015), 56.
11. "Nightingale Pledge," Wikipedia, last modified November 2, 2015, https://en.wikipedia.org/wiki/Nightingale_Pledge.
12. 1 Chronicles 12:32, NLT.
13. The New Living Translation calls them "leaders."
14. Anthony J. Mayo and Nitin Nohria, *In Their Time: The Greatest Business Leaders of the Twentieth Century* (Boston: Harvard Business School, 2005), 5.
15. Matthew 28:19.

16. International Civil Society Centre, "Missing the 'Kodak Moment,'" Disrupt & Innovate, https://disrupt-and-innovate.org/book /facing-disruption/missing-the-kodak-moment/.

17. Peter H. Diamandis and Steven Kotler, *Bold: How to Go Big, Create Wealth, and Impact the World* (New York: Simon & Schuster, 2015), 16.

18. Diamandis and Kotler, *Bold,* 5.

19. R. T. Kendall, *The Anointing: Yesterday, Today, Tomorrow* (Lake Mary, FL: Charisma House, 2003), 44.

20. Kendall, *The Anointing,* 133.

21. "Henri Cartier-Bresson," Wikipedia.

22. "Richard Feynman," Wikipedia, last modified April 26, 2016, https://en.wikipedia.org/wiki/Richard_Feynman.

23. Richard Feynman, "The Making of a Scientist," http://bpsscience.weebly .com/uploads/2/2/1/3/2213712/4.2_feynman_-_the_making_of_a _scientist_close_reading_exemplar.pdf.

24. "How Much Time Does It Take for a 95 M.P.H. Fastball to Reach Home Plate?" PhoenixBats.com, https://www.phoenixbats.com /baseball-bat-infographic.html.

25. David Epstein, *The Sports Gene: Inside the Science of Extraordinary Athletic Performance* (New York: Current, 2014), 5.

26. "Wayne Gretzky," Brainy Quote, www.brainyquote.com/quotes/quotes /w/waynegretz383282.html.

27. Epstein, *The Sports Gene,* 9.

Chapter 7: Frozen

1. Richard Goldstein, "George Shuba, 89, Dies; Handshake Heralded Racial Tolerance in Baseball," September 30, 2014, www.nytimes.com/2014 /10/01/sports/baseball/george-shuba-whose-handshake-heralded-racial -tolerance-in-baseball-dies-at-89.html?_r=0.

2. Roger Kahn, *The Boys of Summer,* reissue ed. (New York: Harper Perennial, 2006), 224.

3. Kahn, *The Boys of Summer,* 241.

4. Jon Gordon, "Will Smith's Secret to Success," *Jon Gordon Blog,* www .jongordon.com/blog/will-smiths-secret-to-success/.

5. 2 Samuel 23:10.

6. Peter King, "I Desperately Want to Be Coached," *Sports Illustrated,* September 9, 2015, http://mmqb.si.com/mmqb/2015/09/09/aaron

-rodgers-mike-mccarthy-tom-clements-green-back-packers-avoiding
-interceptions.

7. "Pablo Casals," https://en.wikipedia.org/wiki/Pablo_Casals.

8. See Deuteronomy 28:2.

9. See Isaiah 55:11.

10. See Jeremiah 1:12.

11. See Philippians 1:6.

12. John Wooden, Good Reads, www.goodreads.com/quotes/175302-make
-each-day-your-masterpiece.

13. "Stream of Consciousness," *Gaiam Life,* http://blog.gaiam.com/quotes
/authors/friedrich-nietzsche?page=2.

14. 1 Samuel 7:12, KJV.

15. See 1 Samuel 17:54, KJV.

16. See 1 Samuel 17:4–7.

17. See Leviticus 23:39.

18. Deuteronomy 24:5.

19. "Let It Go," Wikipedia, last modified April 28, 2016, https://en.wikipedia
.org/wiki/Let_It_Go_%28Disney_song%29.

20. Jackson Truax, "Frozen Composers Robert Lopez and Kristen Anderson-
Lopez," Awards Daily.com, November 27, 2013, www.awardsdaily.com
/2013/11/27/frozen-composers-robert-lopez-and-kristen-anderson-lopez/.

21. Adam Grant, *Originals: How Non-Conformists Move the World* (New
York: Viking, 2016), 36.

22. Patrick Gomez, "5 Things to Know About the Masterminds Behind
Frozen's 'Let It Go,'" *People,* March 16, 2014, www.people.com/people
/article/0,,20797403,00.html.

23. I first came across this idea while reading a biography of Peter Marshall.
It was the test he employed to discern God's will.

Chapter 8: Field of Dreams

1. Check out summitleaders.org.

2. See Genesis 15:5.

3. "Winston Churchill," Brainy Quote, www.brainyquote.com/quotes
/quotes/w/winstonchu136790.html.

4. See Mark 16:20.

5. See Genesis 6.

6. See 2 Kings 3.

7. See 2 Kings 4.

8. I'm not sure who coined that phrase, but John Ortberg has a wonderful book by that title.

Chapter 9: On This Spot

1. Julia Solis, *New York Underground: The Anatomy of a City* (New York: Routledge, 2005), 13–14.
2. William Tindall, *Standard History of the City of Washington: From a Study of the Original Sources* (Knoxville, TN: H. W. Crew, 1914), 9–18.
3. Tindall, *Standard History,* 18.
4. See Genesis 22:1–2 and 2 Chronicles 3:1.
5. Zachary M. Seward, "Recap of 'Serial' Season Two, Episode One: Welcome Back, Old Friend—and Hello, Bowe Bergdahl," December 10, 2015, http://qz.com/570713/recap-of-serial-season-two-episode-one -welcome-back-old-friend-and-hello-bowe-bergdahl/.
6. Eric Weiner, *The Geography of Genius: A Search for the World's Most Creative Places from Ancient Athens to Silicon Valley* (New York: Simon & Schuster, 2016), 2.
7. Psalm 34:3.

Chapter 10: The Lion's Den

1. My father-in-law, Bob Schmidgall, told this story during the message our family listened to on Thanksgiving night 2015. It's dated February 21, 1979.
2. Thanks to Jeffrey Portman for this concept, this challenge. I first heard it from him while speaking at an event in Seattle, Washington.
3. Kirk Cousins, *Game Changer: Faith, Football, and Finding Your Way* (Grand Rapids, MI: Zondervan, 2014), 83.
4. Hebrews 11:32–34.
5. Hebrews 11:35–37.
6. "J. W. Tucker Event," YouTube, October 31, 2007, https://www.youtube .com/watch?v=lOXVofTSIQ0.
7. George O. Wood, submitted by Marshall Shelley, "A Missionary's Sacrifice Was Worth the Cost," *Preaching Today,* www.preaching today.com/illustrations/2008/august/7032706.html.

Chapter 11: Fight Club

1. *The Book of Legends/Sefer Ha-Aggadah: Legends from the Talmud and Midrash*, ed. Hayim Nahman Bialik and Yehoshua Hana Ravnitzky, trans. William G. Braude (New York: Schocken Books, 1992), 128.
2. *The Book of Legends*, 128.
3. See 1 Chronicles 11:23.
4. See Isaiah 54:17.
5. See James 4:7.
6. See Romans 8:31.
7. See 1 John 4:4.
8. Corrie ten Boom with Elizabeth Sherrill and John Sherrill, *The Hiding Place: The Triumphant True Story of Corrie ten Boom* (Grand Rapids, MI: Chosen Books, 2006), 8.
9. Martin Luther King Jr., "Transformed Nonconformist," November 1954, http://okra.stanford.edu/transcription/document_images/Vol06Scans/Nov1954TransformedNonconformist.pdf.
10. King Jr., "Transformed Nonconformist."
11. Rosa Parks with Jim Haskins, *Rosa Parks: My Story* (New York: Puffin Books, 1992), 116.
12. "Rosa Parks: 'I had been pushed as far as I could stand,'" Salon, February 3, 2013, www.salon.com/2013/02/03/rosa_parks_i_had_been_pushed_as_far_as_i_could_stand/.
13. Mark Batterson, *Wild Goose Chase: Reclaim the Adventure of Pursuing God* (Colorado Springs, CO: Multnomah, 2008), 66–67.

Chapter 12: Run to the Roar

1. "Jack Handey Quotes," ThinkExist.com, http://thinkexist.com/quotation/when_you_die-if_you_get_a_choice_between_going_to/340632.html.
2. "Franz Reichelt," Wikipedia, last modified April 28, 2016, https://en.wikipedia.org/wiki/Franz_Reichelt.
3. 2 Timothy 2:15, KJ 2000.
4. Thanks to Jim Collins for this concept, called the Stockdale Paradox, which you can read about in his classic *Good to Great*.
5. 1 John 4:18, ESV.
6. 1 Samuel 21:13.
7. Matthew 16:18, ESV.

8. Neal Roese, *If Only: How to Turn Regret into Opportunity* (New York: Broadway, 2005), 48.

Chapter 13: Snowy Day

1. Bob Ruppert, "The Statue of George III," *Journal of the American Revolution*, September 8, 2014, http://allthingsliberty.com/2014/09 /the-statue-of-george-iii/.
2. Ruppert, "The Statue of George III."
3. See 1 Samuel 15:12.
4. "Compensation," Wikipedia, last modified April 29, 2016, https://en .wikipedia.org/wiki/Compensation_%28psychology%29.
5. Malcolm Gladwell, "The Uses of Adversity," *The New Yorker,* November 10, 2008, www.newyorker.com/magazine/2008/11/10/the-uses-of -adversity.
6. George Bernard Shaw, Good Reads, www.goodreads.com/quotes/39982 -people-are-always-blaming-their-circumstances-for-what-they-are.
7. W. H. Murray, *The Scottish Himalayan Expedition* (London: J. M. Dent and Sons, 1951).
8. Andy Stanley, *Next Generation Leader: 5 Essentials for Those Who Will Shape the Future* (Colorado Springs, CO: Multnomah, 2006), 93.
9. Daniel J. Boorstin, *The Seekers: The Story of Man's Continuing Quest to Understand His World* (New York: Vintage Books, 1999), 278.
10. John 4:35.
11. John 4:35.
12. If all else fails, watch Shia LaBeouf's motivational speech "Just Do It," YouTube, https://www.youtube.com/watch?v=ZXsQAXx_ao0.
13. Christopher Harress, "The Sad End of Blockbuster Video: The Onetime $5 Billion Company Is Being Liquidated as Competition from Online Giants Netflix and Hulu Prove All Too Much for the Iconic Brand," *International Business Times,* December 5, 2013, www.ibtimes.com /sad-end-blockbuster-video-onetime-5-billion-company-being-liquidated -competition-1496962.
14. Joseph Baxter, "Netflix Is Now Worth More Than CBS," www.cinema blend.com/television/Netflix-Now-Worth-More-Than-CBS-71382.html.
15. Adam Grant, *Originals: How Non-Conformists Move the World* (New York: Viking, 2016), 1–2.
16. Grant, *Originals,* 1.

Chapter 14: Five-Pound Dream

1. Check out the coffee farmers at www.redeeminggrounds.com/the-growers/. And while you're there, buy a bag of beans!
2. Genesis 50:20.
3. Genesis 37:19.
4. This idea originated with Erwin McManus.
5. 2 Samuel 23:20, KJV.
6. Luke 6:38.

Chapter 15: Double Destiny

1. Jeremiah 1:4–5.
2. Matthew 19:26.
3. Luke 1:37, ESV.
4. 2 Samuel 23:22.
5. Check out ipourlife.org.
6. See Romans 8:29.
7. Edward Grant Ries, "The True History of William Wallace," www.electricscotland.com/books/ries/TheTrueHistoryof WilliamWallace.pdf.
8. Ries, "The True History."
9. Check out Joshua's book *The President's Devotional: The Daily Readings That Inspired President Obama* (New York: HarperOne, 2013).

Chapter 16: Chain Reaction

1. Lorne Whitehead, "Domino 'Chain Reaction,'" *American Journal of Physics* 51 (1983): 182, http://popperfont.net/2013/01/16/physics-of-the-domino-effect-or-how-to-knock-over-the-empire-state-building-using-28-dominos/.
2. Peter H. Diamandis, "The Difference Between Linear and Exponential Thinking," Big Think, http://bigthink.com/in-their-own-words/the-difference-between-linear-and-exponential-thinking.
3. Whitehead, "Domino 'Chain Reaction.'"
4. Acts 2:39.
5. 1 Kings 19:15–16, NKJV.
6. Doris Kearns Goodwin, *No Ordinary Time: Franklin and Eleanor Roosevelt: The Home Front in World War II* (New York: Simon & Schuster, 1994), 633.

Chapter 17: The Rabbit Room

1. Philip Zaleski and Carol Zaleski, *The Fellowship: The Literary Lives of the Inklings: J. R. R. Tolkien, C. S. Lewis, Owen Barfield, Charles Williams* (New York: Farrar, Straus, and Giroux), 59.
2. Zaleski and Zaleski, *The Fellowship*, 63.
3. To see my full list of life goals, check out *The Circle Maker*.
4. Zaleski and Zaleski, *The Fellowship*, 3.
5. "Paschal Imagination," RonRolheiser, OMI, February 18, 1991, http://ronrolheiser.com/paschal-imagination/#.Vz3DV2ZmiiU.
6. Zaleski and Zaleski, *The Fellowship*, 198.
7. Zaleski and Zaleski, *The Fellowship*, 26.
8. See 1 Corinthians 15:33.

Chapter 18: Counternarratives

1. Stephen Mansfield, *Mansfield's Book of Manly Men: An Utterly Invigorating Guide to Being Your Most Masculine Self* (Nashville, TN: Thomas Nelson, 2013), 214.
2. Johnson Brigham, *Des Moines: The Pioneer of Municipal Progress and Reform of the Middle West* (Chicago: S. J. Clarke Publishing, 1911), 1:631–32, https://books.google.com/books?id=qdRCAQAAMAAJ&pg=PA631&lpg=PA631&dq=booker+t+washington+Des+Moines+hotel&source=bl&ots=OZJoHWsd4I&sig=qROq3J-i05NfKOidN33zWWxKexE&hl=en&sa=X&ved=0CDgQ6AEwAmoVChMIwJvsqq_MxwIVQjw-Ch0-5gQ2#v=onepage&q=booker%20t%20washington%20Des%20Moines%20hotel&f=false.
3. Mansfield, *Mansfield's Book of Manly Men*, 214.
4. Matthew 6:1–2.
5. James O'Shea, "Chuck Feeney, Unsung Hero, Honored by IrishCentral, Guinness," IrishCentral, August 6, 2014, www.irishcentral.com/culture/Chuck-Feeney-Unsung-Hero-honored-by-IrishCentral-Guinness.html.
6. Steven Bertoni, "Chuck Feeney: The Billionaire Who Is Trying to Go Broke," *Forbes*, October 8, 2012, www.forbes.com/sites/stevenbertoni/2012/09/18/chuck-feeney-the-billionaire-who-is-trying-to-go-broke/.
7. Matthew 6:3–4.
8. See Ezekiel 37.
9. Check out http://mananutrition.org/.
10. Revelation 2:17.

11. Alex Haley, Brainy Quote, www.brainyquote.com/quotes/quotes/a/alex haley388531.html.
12. Vince Lombardi Jr., Good Reads, www.goodreads.com/quotes/19425 -the-man-on-top-of-the-mountain-didn-t-fall-there.

Chapter 19: The Thirteenth Virtue
1. Proverbs 22:29, KJV.
2. Walter Isaacson, *Benjamin Franklin: An American Life* (New York: Simon & Schuster, 2003), 12.
3. "Washington's Aides-De-Camp," Wikipedia, last modified February 13, 2016, https://en.wikipedia.org/wiki/Washington%27s_Aides-de-Camp.
4. Evan Kirkpatrick, "Launching a Non-Profit? Here Is the Best Advice from 6 Leading Social Entrepreneurs," *Forbes*, November 23, 2015, www.forbes .com/sites/evankirkpatrick/2015/11/23/launching-a-non-profit-here -is-the-best-advice-from-7-leading-social-entrepreneurs/4/.
5. Isaacson, *Benjamin Franklin*, 41.
6. Check out NCC worship at nccworship.net.
7. See www.whatisorange.org/.
8. Proverbs 16:18, KJV; 18:12.
9. 2 Samuel 23:23.

Chapter 20: A Hundred Years from Now
1. "Guinness Brewery," Wikipedia, last modified March 28, 2016, https://en.wikipedia.org/wiki/Guinness_Brewery.
2. Stephen Mansfield, *The Search for God and Guinness: A Biography of the Beer That Changed the World* (Nashville: Thomas Nelson, 2009), 258.
3. "George Washington before the Battle of Long Island," Thirty-Thousand .org, www.thirty-thousand.org/pages/Free_Men.htm.
4. William Eleroy Curtis, *The True Abraham Lincoln* (Philadelphia: J. B. Lippincott, 1902), 176.
5. "George Washington before the Battle."
6. Psalm 78:6.
7. Dan Van Veen, "AG, Church Share 90th Anniversary," Assemblies of God, January 19, 2005, http://ag.org/top/News/index_articledetail.cfm?Process =DisplayArticle&targetBay=c97d4d5c-a325-4921-9a9e-e9fbddd9cdce &ModID=2&RSS_RSSContentID=3510&RSS_OriginatingChannel ID=1184&RSS_OriginatingRSSFeedID=3359&RSS_Source=search.

8. Stanley Tam made this comment over dinner after speaking at National Community Church.

9. "Pancake, Pankake, Panique, Kaniess, Saar, Ovitt and Related Families," Roots Web, last updated February 5, 2015, http://wc.rootsweb.ancestry .com/cgi-bin/igm.cgi?op=GET&db=pankake&id=I2221.

10. Matthew 1:6, KJ 2000.

11. "St. Crispin's Day Speech," Wikipedia, last modified April 16, 2016, https://en.wikipedia.org/wiki/St_Crispin's_Day_Speech.

ARIADNE'S THREAD

In Greek mythology, there is a legend about a labyrinth that was unnavigable and inescapable. No one who entered ever exited. Not only was the maze incredibly complex, but within it meandered a Minotaur, a fearsome creature that was half man, half bull. Every nine years, the evil king of Crete demanded that the Athenians send a tribute of seven boys and seven girls to be sacrificed to the Minotaur. As you might imagine, the Athenians did not take well to this tradition.

On the occasion of the third Minotaur Games, the king of Athens, Theseus, volunteered himself as tribute in place of his young citizens. When King Theseus landed on Crete, the daughter of the Cretan king, Princess Ariadne, fell head over ancient heels in love with him. She knew that no one who had ventured into the labyrinth had ever found their way out, so she devised a rather ingenious plan. Ariadne gave Theseus a sword with which to slay the Minotaur and, more importantly, a ball of thread. After tying one end to the entrance, Theseus unwound the ball of thread as he wove his way through the spiderweb of corridors. After successfully slaying the Minotaur, Theseus was able to moonwalk his way out of the labyrinth with the help of Ariadne's thread.*

Life is a labyrinth, is it not? It's full of relational twists and occupational turns we couldn't see coming. We zig through big decisions and zag through bad ones. There are situations we get ourselves into that we don't know how

---

* *Encyclopaedia Britannica Online,* s.v. "Ariadne," www.britannica.com/topic/Ariadne-Greek
-mythology.

to get ourselves out of. And we all encounter some Minotaurs along the way—you may even work for one.

As we weave our way through difficult seasons and difficult decisions, we might feel as helpless and hopeless as if trying to escape an ancient labyrinth, but there is a way out. There is a ball of thread, but to follow it involves some backtracking.

In fact, we've got to go all the way back to the very beginning.

Ancient Instinct

The Austrian psychologist Alfred Adler was famous for beginning counseling sessions with new clients by asking, "What is your earliest memory?" No matter how the patient replied, Adler responded, "And so life is."*

Adler believed that our earliest memories leave a profound imprint on our souls. For better or worse, it can be difficult to escape their gravitational pull. Our earliest memories have unusual staying power.

Imagine Alfred Adler sitting down with Adam and asking his trademark question: What is your earliest memory? Adam's answer would not refer to naming the animals or rib surgery. It would not allude to the serpent's temptation or the awkwardness of nakedness after succumbing to it. Adam's earliest memory?

> God blessed them and said, "Be fruitful and multiply. Fill the earth
> and govern it. Reign over the fish in the sea, the birds in the sky, and
> all the animals that scurry along the ground."†

Did you catch that? Adam's earliest memory would've been receiving blessing from God. Blessing sets the tone, sets the table. It establishes Adam's emotional baseline. It kick-starts Adam's spiritual trend line. And not

---

* Mark Batterson, *Soulprint: Discovering Your Divine Destiny* (Colorado Springs: Multnomah, 2011), 57.
† Genesis 1:28, NLT.

only is God's blessing Adam's earliest memory, but it's also God's most ancient instinct. The blessing of God is Ariadne's thread.

Do you know what is one of the most repeated words in the Old Testament? I've tipped my cards, so you can probably venture a guess. The answer is the Hebrew word *barak*. That Hebrew word has a plethora of meanings, which we'll unpack. But the most common translation is "blessing."* It's the word employed in God's original blessing, but it's more than the opening act. It's the central storyline of Scripture from start to finish.

Have you ever heard of a "tag cloud"?

A tag cloud is a visual representation of textual data. I'm guessing you've seen one before. It's a unique way of weighting the importance of words by color and font size. If you could create a tag cloud of the Old Testament, I'm not sure there is a word that is bigger or brighter than *blessing*! Be honest, that's a little surprising given the high volume of brutality and bloodshed before Christ. But there it is, the blessing of God, hidden in plain sight.

Original Blessing

God wants to bless you beyond your ability to ask or imagine.

There, I said it.

I'm not sure what your earliest memory is, good or bad. But for many, memories of their earthly father do not mirror Adam's earliest memory of his heavenly Father. In fact, you may feel cursed rather than blessed by your family of origin. If that's true, if that's you, it can be very difficult to conceive of a heavenly Father whose deepest desire is to bless you. Believe it or not, *God has blessings for you in categories you cannot even conceive of.* If you're going to live a happy, healthy, and holy life, you've got to get that in your gut. That's who God is. That's what God does. As children of God, blessing is our birthright.

---

* Blue Letter Bible, s.v. "blessing," www.blueletterbible.org/lang/lexicon/lexicon.cfm?t=kjv&strongs
=h1288. https://www.blueletterbible.org/lang/lexicon/lexicon.cfm?t=kjv&strongs=h1288.

Now I know what you may be thinking. Am I promising health, wealth, and prosperity? The answer is an unequivocal *no*! God promises us something so much better than physical health or material wealth. And for the record, some of God's greatest blessings are blessings in disguise. The blessing of God is not an immunity card.

Jesus said, "In this world you will have trouble." And Jesus certainly faced His fair share of earthly troubles, including the cross.

But this passage doesn't end with "trouble." Don't put a period where God puts a comma! In the same breath, Jesus said, "But take heart! I have overcome the world."* There are sacrifices to be made, no doubt. There is suffering to endure, no question. But there is a blessing on the other side, a double blessing.

I had better add this: God doesn't bless disobedience! God doesn't bless pride or greed or laziness either! We've got to position ourselves for God's blessing, and that's part of what this book is all about. But make no mistake about it—God has postured Himself to bless you from the very beginning.

The blessing of God is difficult to quantify or qualify. It is both tangible and intangible. It's timely yet timeless. The blessing of God is universally offered to everyone, but it's as unique as your fingerprint.

In *Double Blessing,* we'll explore seven of God's blessings. There are many more, to be sure. But seven is a good starting point. Some of those blessings may be quite familiar, but I'll try to turn the kaleidoscope and show you new ways of looking at them. Other blessings are more obscure, such as "the favor of him who dwelt in the burning bush."† Some blessings are simple and straightforward, while others are more difficult to discern, like the blessing of brokenness.

The blessing of God is the solution to your biggest problem.
The blessing of God is the answer to your boldest prayer.
The blessing of God is the fulfillment of your bravest dream.

---

* John 16:33.
† Deuteronomy 33:16.

After exploring these seven blessings, we'll learn how to flip the blessing. Simply put, we are blessed to bless. The end goal is not to *get* the blessing. The end goal is to *be* the blessing. That's how blessings turn into double blessings. It's by becoming a bigger blessing to those around us that we steward our gifts, consecrate our circumstances, and create our futures. It's the way we pay it back and pay it forward. When we become the blessing, a domino effect is created that reaches across nations and generations.

Journey of Blessing

Before we go any further, let me take you on a little tour de force of blessing from Genesis to Revelation. Remember, the first end of Ariadne's thread must be tied to the original blessing: "Be fruitful and multiply." The blessing of God then weaves its way from the Garden of Eden to Ur of Chaldees where God establishes a covenant of blessing with Abram, a covenant we have been grafted into via a grandfather clause.* The blessing of God survives a soap opera known as Isaac and Jacob, proving itself bigger and better and stronger than any mistake we can make.

During four hundred years of enslavement in Egypt, the blessing survives unspeakable suffering and indescribable setbacks. The blessing finds its voice at a burning bush on the backside of the desert and gives a man named Moses the courage to confront the Pharaoh. On the eve of the Exodus, the blessing of God is the blood of the Passover lamb that provides a hedge of protection for God's people. During Israel's wanderings, the blessing becomes a cloud by day that gives shade and a fire by night that gives light.

While in the wilderness, a priestly blessing is pronounced on the people of God from the summit of Mount Gerizim.† The priestly blessing becomes a kingly blessing, weaving its way through a shepherd's field, a fugitive's cave, and into King David's throne room. The blessing finds it's true fulfillment a

---

* Romans 11:11–24.
† Deuteronomy 27:12.

thousand years later in the Son of David, in the City of David. The blessing of God is birthed in Bethlehem, God with us.

The blessing seems to take a wrong turn through the Garden of Gethsemane, down the Via Dolorosa, all the way to a dead end known as "the place of the Skull."* The blessing of God redeemed us from the curse of the law at Calvary's cross, God for us.

The covenant of blessing turned into the cup of blessing, the bottomless cup of God's grace from which we drink every time we come to the Lord's Table and celebrate our communion with Christ. The blessing was signed, sealed, and delivered on the third day. With it, a fine-print footnote the Father had not forgotten: "I will give you the sacred blessings I promised to David."†

At His ascension, the very last thing Jesus did was to bless His disciples. Forty days later, on the Day of Pentecost, a second blessing was bestowed on the disciples in an upper room. The Holy Spirit manifests gifts and produces fruit. The Spirit of God also seals our salvation, God in us.

Finally, we arrive at the end of God's revelation, and it's just the beginning of blessing. God's most ancient instinct finds its eternal expression. It's there that we tie the other end of Ariadne's thread to the last blessing in the Bible, the eternal blessing.

> Blessed are those who wash their robes, that they may have the right
> to the tree of life and may go through the gates into the city.‡

In this book, we'll pull the thread of God's blessing all the way from Genesis to Revelation. My prayer is that it will find its genesis in your life and that you'll have a greater revelation of both the blessing God has for you and the blessing He wants you to become.

---

* John 19:17.
† Acts 13:34, NLT.
‡ Revelation 22:14.

Pulling at the Thread

During Israel's captivity in the sixth century BC, the blessing of God must have seemed as far away as Babylon was from Jerusalem. But the prophet Zechariah doesn't refer to God's people as prisoners of war. He calls them "prisoners of hope."

If you find yourself in similar circumstances, if you feel more cursed than blessed, you've got to pitch your tent in the land of hope.* I cannot promise that God will deliver you *from* your circumstances, but He will never leave you nor forsake you. And He who began a good work will carry it to completion. Not only will God deliver you *through* them, but there is also double blessing on the other side.

I will restore to you double.†

I recognize that this promise was given to a unique people in unique circumstances. And I would counsel against turning it into a mathematical ratio, but it does reveal the heart of God. He doesn't just redeem what the Enemy has stolen; He adds interest. In this instance, two hundred percent.

The first half of *Double Blessing* is about positioning ourselves for God's blessing. Once you get the blessing, it's all about becoming the blessing. The second half of this book will focus on flipping the blessing, and that starts with identifying how and where and when you have been blessed.

At times, the blessing of God is awfully hard to see. You may feel like the blessing is buried or hiding. Or maybe you feel as though the thread of blessing has been broken because of mistakes you make. I believe that God is going to thread the needle through this book and turn your life into a bigger blessing than you could have asked or imagined.

---

* Acts 2:26, MSG.
† Zechariah 9:12, ESV.

Find the Courage to Chase the Lions in Your Life

The *Chase the Lion Weekly Planner* is the essential companion for recognizing and achieving your goals! Designed to be started at any point during the year, this undated weekly planner will encourage you to stay organized with motivational tools and exercises, including:

- monthly calendars
- weekly planning spreads
- blank journal pages
- instructions on creating your own Lion Chaser's manifesto
- space to record your top one hundred life goals
- year-at-a-glance calendars for multiple years

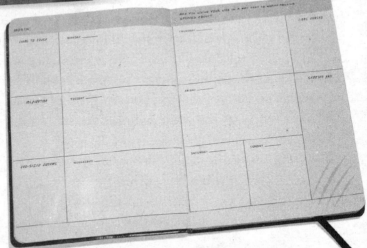

With this strategic planning tool, you can find the courage to chase the lions in your life and go after your God-ordained destiny!

www.ChaseTheLion.com